Bayesian Nonparametrics via Neural Networks

ASA-SIAM Series on Statistics and Applied Probability

The ASA-SIAM Series on Statistics and Applied Probability is published jointly by the American Statistical Association and the Society for Industrial and Applied Mathematics. The series consists of a broad spectrum of books on topics in statistics and applied probability. The purpose of the series is to provide inexpensive, quality publications of interest to the intersecting membership of the two societies.

Editorial Board

Bayesian Nonparametrics via Neural Networks

Herbert K. H. Lee

University of California, Santa Cruz
Santa Cruz, California

Society for Industrial and Applied Mathematics
Philadelphia, Pennsylvania

American Statistical Association
Alexandria, Virginia

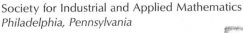

This research was supported in part by the National Science Foundation (grants DMS 9803433, 9873275, and 0233710) and the National Institutes of Health (grant RO1 CA54852-08).

Library of Congress Cataloging-in-Publication Data

Lee, Herbert K. H.
    Bayesian nonparametrics via neural networks / Herbert K.H. Lee.
       p. cm. — (ASA-SIAM series on statistics and applied probability)
    Includes bibliographical references and index.
    ISBN 0-89871-563-6 (pbk.)
     1. Bayesian statistical decision theory. 2. Nonparametric statistics. 3. Neural networks (Computer science) I. Title. II. Series.

    QA279.5.L43 2004
    519.5'42—dc22
                                      2004048151

A portion of the royalties from the sale of this book are being placed in a fund to help students attend SIAM meetings and other SIAM-related activities. This fund is administered by SIAM and qualified individuals are encouraged to write directly to SIAM for guidelines.

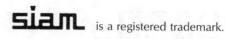 is a registered trademark.

Contents

List of Figures

Preface

When I first heard about neural networks and how great they were, I was rather skeptical. Being sold as a magical black box, there was enough hype to make one believe that they could solve the world's problems. When I tried to learn more about them, I found that most of the literature was written for a machine learning audience, and I had to grapple with a new perspective and a new set of terminology. After some work, I came to see neural networks from a statistical perspective, as a probability model. One of the primary motivations for this book was to write about neural networks for statisticians, addressing issues and concerns of interest to statisticians, and using statistical terminology. Neural networks are a powerful model, and should be treated as such, rather than disdained as a "mere algorithm" as I have found some statisticians do. Hopefully this book will prove to be illuminating.

The phrase "Bayesian nonparametrics" means different things to different people. The traditional interpretation usually implies infinite dimensional processes such as Dirichlet processes, used for problems in regression, classification, and density estimation. While on the surface this book may not appear to fit that description, it is actually close. One of the themes of this book is that a neural network can be viewed as a finite-dimensional approximation to an infinite-dimensional model, and that this model is useful in practice for problems in regression and classification.

Thus the first section of this book will focus on introducing neural networks within the statistical context of nonparametric regression and classification. The rest of the book will examine important statistical modeling issues for Bayesian neural networks, particularly the choice of prior and the choice of model.

While this book will not assume the reader has any prior knowledge about neural networks, neither will it try to be an all-inclusive introduction. Topics will be introduced in a self-contained manner, with references provided for further details of the many issues that will not be directly addressed in this book.

The target audience for this book is practicing statisticians and researchers, as well as students preparing for either or both roles. This book addresses practical and theoretical issues. It is hoped that the users of neural networks will want an understanding of how the model works, which can lead to a better appreciation of knowing when it is working and when it is not. It will be assumed that the reader has already been introduced to the basics of the Bayesian approach, with only a brief review and additional references provided. There are a number of good introductory books on Bayesian statistics available (see Section 2.4), so it does not seem productive to repeat that material here. It will also be assumed that the reader has a solid background in mathematical statistics and in linear regression, such as that which would be acquired as part of a traditional Master's degree in statistics. However, there are few formal proofs, and much of the text should be accessible even without this background. Computational issues will be discussed at conceptual and algorithmic levels.

This work developed from my Ph.D. thesis ("Model Selection and Model Averaging for Neural Networks", Carnegie Mellon University, Department of Statistics, 1998). I am grateful for all the assistance and knowledge provided by my advisor, Larry Wasserman. I would also like to acknowledge the many individuals who have contributed to this effort, including David Banks, Jim Berger, Roberto Carta, Merlise Clyde, Daniel Cork, Scott Davies, Sigrunn Eliassen, Chris Genovese, Robert Gramacy, Rob Kass, Milovan Krnjajić, Meena Mani, Daniel Merl, Andrew Moore, Peter Müller, Mark Schervish, Valerie Ventura, and Kert Viele, as well as the staff at SIAM and a number of anonymous referees and editors, both for this book and for the papers preceding it. At various points during this work, funding has been provided by the National Science Foundation (grants DMS 9803433, 9873275, and 0233710) and the National Institutes of Health (grant RO1 CA54852-08).

Chapter 1

Introduction

The goal of this book is to put neural network models firmly into a statistical framework, treating them with the accompanying rigor normally accorded to statistical models. A neural network is frequently seen as either a magical black box, or purely as a machine learning algorithm, when in fact there is a definite probability model behind it. This book will start by showing how neural networks are indeed a statistical model for doing nonparametric regression or classification. The focus will be on a Bayesian perspective, although many of the topics will apply to frequentist models as well. As much of the literature on neural networks appears in the computer science realm, many standard modeling questions fail to get addressed. In particular, this book will take a hard look at key modeling issues such as choosing an appropriate prior and dealing with model selection. Most of the existing literature deals with neural networks as an algorithm. The hope of this book is to shift the focus back to modeling.

1.1 Statistics and Machine Learning

The fields of statistics and machine learning are two approaches toward the same goals, with much in common. In both cases, the idea is to learn about a problem from data. In most cases, this is either a classification problem, a regression problem, an exploratory data analysis problem, or some combination of the above. Where statistics and machine learning differ most is in their perspective. It is sort of like two people, one standing outside of an airplane, and one standing inside the same plane, both asked to describe this plane. The person outside might discuss the length, the wingspan, the number of engines and their layout, and so on. The person inside might comment on the number of rows of seats, the number of aisles, the seat configurations, the amount of overhead storage space, the number of lavatories, and so on. In the end, they are both describing the same plane. The relationship between statistics and machine learning is much like this situation. As much of the terminology differs between the two fields, towards the end of this book a glossary is provided for translating relevant machine learning terms into statistical terms.

As a bit of an overgeneralization, the field of statistics and the methods that come out of it are based on probability models. At the heart of almost all analyses, there is some distribution describing a random quantity, and the methodology springs from the probability model. For example, in simple linear regression, we relate the response y to the explanatory variable x via the conditional distribution $y \sim N(\beta_0 + \beta_1 x, \sigma^2)$ using possibly unknown parameters β_0, β_1, and σ^2. The core of the model is the probability model.

For a matching overgeneralization, machine learning can be seen as the art of developing algorithms for learning from data. The idea is to devise a clever algorithm that will perform well in practice. It is a pragmatic approach that has produced many useful tools for data analysis.

Many individual data analysis methods are associated only with the field in which they were developed. In some cases, methods have been invented in one field and reinvented in the other, with the terminology remaining completely different, and the research remaining separate. This is unfortunate, since both fields have much to learn from each other. It is like the airplane example, where a more complete description of the plane is available when both observers cooperate.

Traditionally, neural networks are seen as a machine learning algorithm. They were largely developed by the machine learning community (or the precursor community, artificial intelligence); see Section 2.3.2. In most implementations, the focus is on prediction, using the neural network as a means of finding good predictions, i.e., as an algorithm. Yet a neural network is also a statistical model. Chapter 2 will show how it is simply another method for nonparametric regression or classification. There is an underlying probability model, and, with the proper perspective, a neural network is seen as a generalization of linear regression. Further discussion is found in Section 2.3.1.

For a more traditional approach to neural networks, the reader is referred to Bishop (1995) or Ripley (1996), two excellent books that are statistically accurate but have somewhat of a machine learning perspective. Fine (1999) is more statistical in flavor but mostly non-Bayesian. Several good (but not Bayesian) statistical review articles are also available (Cheng and Titterington (1994); Stern (1996); Warner and Misra (1996)). A final key reference is Neal (1996), which details a fully Bayesian approach to neural networks from a perspective that combines elements from both machine learning and statistics.

1.2   Outline of the Book

This section is meant to give the reader an idea of where this book is going from here. The next two sections of this chapter will introduce two data examples that will be used throughout the book, one for regression and one for classification. The final section of this chapter gives a brief introduction to a simple neural network model, to provide some concreteness to the concept of a neural network, before moving on. Chapter 2 provides a statistical context for neural networks, showing how they fit into the larger framework of nonparametric regression and classification. It will also give a brief review of the Bayesian approach and of concepts in model building. Chapter 3 will focus on choosing a prior, which is a key item in a Bayesian analysis. Also included are details on model fitting and a result on posterior asymptotic consistency. Chapter 4 gets into the nuts and bolts of model building, discussing model selection and alternatives such as model averaging, both at conceptual and implementational levels.

1.3 Regression Example—Groundlevel Ozone Pollution

An example that will be used throughout this book to illustrate a problem in nonparametric regression is a dataset on groundlevel ozone pollution. This dataset first appeared in Breiman and Friedman (1985) and was analyzed extensively by Hastie and Tibshirani (1990). Other authors have also used this dataset, so it is useful to be able to compare results from methods in this book with other published results.

The data consist of groundlevel ozone measurements in the Los Angeles area over the course of a year, along with other meteorological variables. The goal is to use the meteorological covariates to predict ozone concentration, which is a pollutant at the level of human activity. The version of the data used here is that in Hastie and Tibshirani (1990), with missing data removed, so that there are complete measurements for 330 days in 1976. For each of these days, the response variable of interest is the daily maximum one-hour-average ozone level in parts per million at Upland, California. Also available are nine possible explanatory variables: VH, the altitude at which the pressure is 500 millibars; WIND, the wind speed (mph) at Los Angeles International Airport (LAX); HUM, the humidity (%) at LAX; TEMP, the temperature (degrees F) at Sandburg Air Force Base; IBH, the temperature inversion base height (feet); DPG, the pressure gradient (mm Hg) from LAX to Daggert; IBT, the inversion base temperature (degrees F) at LAX; VIS, the visibility (miles) at LAX; and DAY, the day of the year (numbered from 1 to 365).

The data are displayed in pairwise scatterplots in Figure 1.1. The first thing to notice is that most variables have a strong nonlinear association with the ozone level, making prediction feasible but requiring a flexible model to capture the nonlinear relationship. Fitting a generalized additive model (GAM, local smoothed functions for each variable without interaction effects), as described in Section 2.1.1 or in Hastie and Tibshirani (1990), produces the fitted relationships between the explanatory variables (rescaled to the unit interval) and ozone displayed in Figure 1.2. Most variables display a strong relationship with ozone, and all but the first are clearly nonlinear. This problem is thus an example of nonparametric regression, in that some smoothing of the data is necessary, but we must determine how much smoothing is optimal. We will apply neural networks to this problem and compare the results to other nonparametric techniques.

Another notable feature of this dataset is that many variables are highly related to each other, for example VH, TEMP, and IBT, as can be seen in Figure 1.1. It is important to deal with this multicollinearity to avoid overfitting and reduce the variance of predictions. The favored approaches in this book include selection and model averaging. We shall see that neural networks perform well when compared to existing methods in the literature.

1.4 Classification Example—Loan Applications

As an example of a classification problem, a dataset that we shall revisit comes from consumer banking. One question of interest is classifying loan applications for acceptance or rejection. The high correlation between explanatory variables presents certain challenges. There is also direct interest in the problem of model selection, as will be explained below.

Historically, banking was a local and personal operation. When a customer wanted a loan, they went to their local bank branch, where they knew the staff, and they applied for

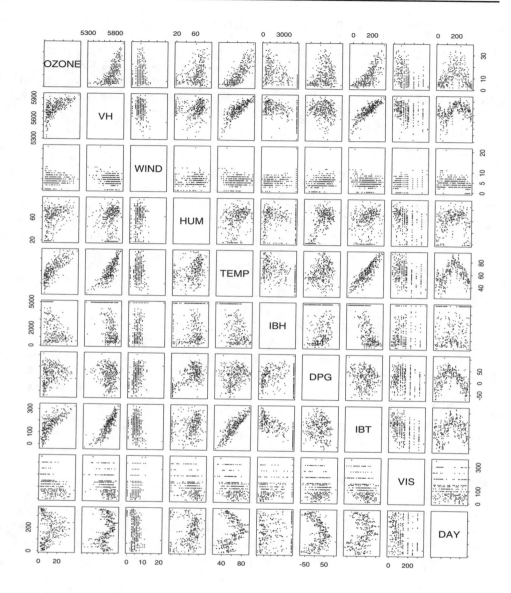

Figure 1.1. *Pairwise scatterplots for the ozone data.*

a loan. The branch manager would then approve or deny the loan based on a combination of the information in the application and their personal knowledge of the customer. As banking grew in scale, the processing of loan applications moved to centralized facilities and was done by trained loan officers who specialized in making such decisions. The personal connection was gone, but there was still a human looking over each application and making his or her decision based on his or her experience as a loan officer. Recently,

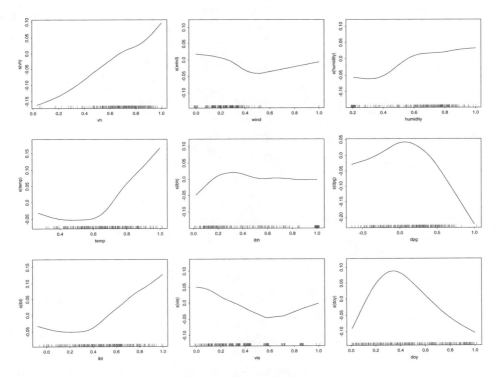

Figure 1.2. *Estimated smooths for the ozone data.*

banks have been switching to partially or completely automated systems for dealing with most loan applications, basing their decisions on algorithms derived from statistical models. This process has been met with much resistance from the loan officers, who believe that the automated processes will mishandle the nonstandard items on many applications, and who are also worried about losing their jobs.

A regional bank wanted to streamline this process, while retaining the human decision element. In particular, the bank wanted to find out what information on the application was most important, so that it could greatly simplify the form, making life easier for the customer and creating cost savings for the bank. Thus the primary goal here is one of variable selection. In the process, one must find a model that predicts well, but the ultimate goal is to find a subset of explanatory variables that is hopefully not too large and can be used to predict as accurately as possible. Even from a statistical standpoint of prediction, any model would need to be concerned with the large amount of correlation between explanatory variables, so model selection would be of interest to help deal with the multicollinearity. We turn to nonparametric models for classification in the hope that by maximizing the flexibility of the model structure, we can minimize the number of covariates necessary for a good fit. In some sections of this book, we will focus on the intermediate goal of predicting whether the loan was actually approved or denied by a human loan officer. In other sections, we will be more concerned with variable selection. This dataset involves the following 23 covariates:

1. Birthdate

2. Length of time in current residence

3. Length of time in previous residence

4. Length of time at current employer

5. Length of time at previous employer

6. Line utilization of available credit

7. Number of inquiries on credit file

8. Date of oldest entry in credit file

9. Income

10. Residential status

11. Monthly mortgage payments

12. Number of checking accounts at this bank

13. Number of credit card accounts at this bank

14. Number of personal credit lines at this bank

15. Number of installment loans at this bank

16. Number of accounts at credit unions

17. Number of accounts at other banks

18. Number of accounts at finance companies

19. Number of accounts at other financial institutions

20. Budgeted debt expenses

21. Amount of loan approved

22. Loan type code

23. Presence of a co-applicant

These variables fall mainly into three groups: stability, demographic, and financial. Stability variables include such items as the length of time the applicant has worked in his or her current job. Stability is thought to be positively correlated with intent and ability to repay a loan; for example, a person who has held a given job longer is less likely to lose it and the corresponding income and be unable to repay a loan. A person who has lived in his or her current residence for longer is less likely to skip town suddenly, leaving behind an unpaid loan. Demographic variables include items like age. In the United States,

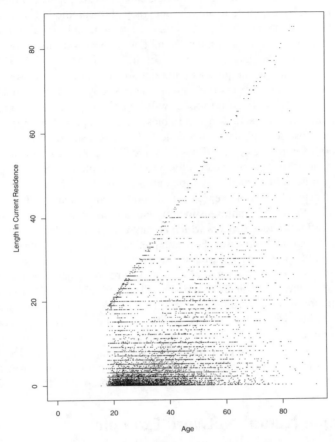

Figure 1.3. *Correlated variables: Age vs. current residence for loan applicants.*

it is illegal to discriminate against older people, but younger people can be discriminated against. Many standard demographic variables (e.g., gender) are not legal for use in a loan decision process and are thus not included. Financial variables include the number of other accounts at this bank and at other financial institutions, as well as the applicant's income and budgeted expenses, and are of obvious interest to a loan officer. The particular loans involved are unsecured (no collateral) personal loans, such as a personal line of credit or a vacation loan.

The covariates in this dataset are highly correlated. In some cases, there is even causation. For example, someone with a mortgage will be a homeowner. Another example is that a person cannot have lived in their current residence for more years than they are old. Figure 1.3 shows a plot of age versus length of time the applicant has reported living in their current residence. Clearly all points must fall below the 45-degree line. Any statistical analysis must take this correlation into account, and model selection is an ideal approach.

A standard approach in the machine learning literature is to split the data into two sets, a *training set*, which is used for fitting the model, and a *test set* for which the fitted model makes predictions, and one then compares the accuracy of the predictions to the true values. Since the loan dataset contains 8508 cases, this is large enough to split into a training set of 4000 observations and a test set of the remaining 4508 observations. 4000 observations are enough to fit complex models, and the test set allows one to see if the fitted model is overfitting (fitting the training set quite well but not able to fit the test set well), or if it can predict well on out-of-sample observations, which is typically the desired goal.

This is a messy dataset, and no model will be able to predict with great accuracy on cases outside the training set. Most variables are self-reported, so there is potential measurement error for the explanatory variables. There is also arbitrary rounding in the self-reporting. For example, residence times are typically reported to the nearest month for short times but to the nearest year or nearest five years for people who have lived in the same place for a longer time. This structure is apparent in Figure 1.3, where the horizontal lines in the picture correspond to whole years near the bottom and clearly delineate every five years in the middle. Some information is incomplete, and there are a number of subjective factors known to influence loan officers which are not coded in the data, so that one cannot hope for too precise a fit on this dataset. For example, data on co-applicants was incomplete, and it was not possible to use those variables because of the very large amount of missing data for cases where there was known to be a co-applicant. A trained loan officer can make much better sense of the incomplete co-applicant data, and this is likely a source of some of the error in the models that will be seen in this book. From talking to loan officers, it seems that the weight given to the presence and the attributes of a co-applicant seem to be based largely on factors that are not easily quantified, such as the reliability of the income source of the primary applicant (e.g., some fields of self-employment are deemed "better" than others, and some employers are known for having more or less employee turnover; an applicant in a less stable job would have more need for a co-applicant).

1.5   A Simple Neural Network Example

In this section, the basic idea of a neural network is introduced via a simple example. More details about neural networks will appear in the following chapters. In particular, Chapter 2 will demonstrate how neural networks can be viewed as a nonparametric model and give some history, and Chapter 3 will explain the interpretation, and lack thereof, of the parameters in the model, as well as methods for fitting the model.

For the ozone data introduced in Section 1.3, consider fitting a model relating ozone levels to the day of the year (coded as 1 through 365). A possible fitted model would be a neural network with two nodes, and one example of such a fit appears in Figure 1.4. The fitted line in the plot is

$$y = 7.13 + \frac{10.58}{1.0 + \exp(21.75 - 0.19 * x)} - \frac{13.12}{1.0 + \exp(19.60 - 0.07 * x)} . \qquad (1.1)$$

How can we make sense of this equation? Neural networks are typically thought of in terms of their "hidden nodes." This is best illustrated with a picture. Figure 1.5 displays our simple model, with a single explanatory variable (day of year), and two hidden nodes.

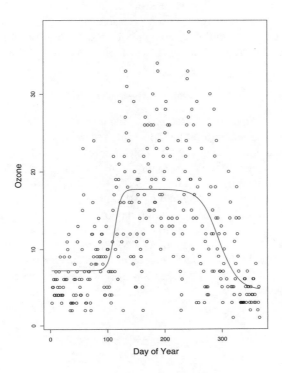

Figure 1.4. *A neural network fitted function.*

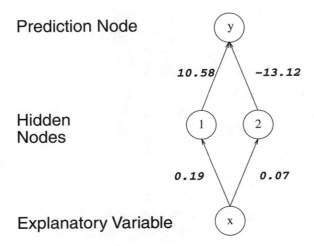

Figure 1.5. *Simple neural network model diagram.*

Starting at the bottom of the diagram, the explanatory variable (input node) feeds its value to each of the hidden nodes, which then transform it and feed those results to the prediction (output) node, which combines them to give the fitted value at the top. In particular, what each hidden node does is to multiply the value of the explanatory variable by a scalar parameter (b), add a scalar (a), and then take the logistic transformation of it:

$$\Psi(x) = \frac{1}{1 + \exp(-a - b*x)} \ . \tag{1.2}$$

So in equation (1.1), the first node has $a = -21.75$ and $b = 0.19$. The b coefficients are shown as the labels of the edges from the input node to the hidden nodes in Figure 1.5 (a is not shown). The prediction node then takes a linear combination of the results of all of the hidden nodes to produce the fitted value. In the figure, the linear coefficients for the hidden nodes are the labels of the edges from the hidden nodes to the prediction node. Returning to equation (1.1), the first node is weighted by 10.58, the second by -13.12, and then 7.13 is added. This results in a fitted value for each day of the year. To make a bit more sense of the plot, note that $\frac{21.75}{0.19} = 114$ is the inflection point for the first rise in the graph, and this occurs when $-a - b*x = 0$ in equation (1.2). So the first rise is the action of the first hidden node. Similarly, the fitted function decreases because of the second hidden node, where the center of the decrease is around $280 = \frac{19.60}{0.07}$. We will return to the interpretations of the parameters in Chapter 3.

Chapter 2

Nonparametric Models

Most standard statistical techniques are *parametric* methods, meaning that a particular family of models, indexed by one or more parameters, is chosen for the data, and the model is fit by choosing optimal values for the parameters (or finding their posterior distribution). Examples include linear regression (with slope and intercept parameters) and logistic regression (with the parameters being the coefficients). In these cases, it is assumed that the choice of model family (e.g., a linear relationship with independent Gaussian error) is the correct family, and all that needs to be done is to fit the coefficients.

The idea behind nonparametric modeling is to move beyond restricting oneself to a particular family of models, instead utilizing a much larger model space. For example, the goal of many nonparametric regression problems is to find the continuous function that best approximates the random process without overfitting the data. In this case, one is not restricted to linear functions, or even differentiable functions. The model is thus *nonparametric* in the sense that the set of possible models under consideration does not belong to a family that can be indexed by a finite number of parameters.

In practice, instead of working directly with an infinite-dimensional space, such as the space of continuous functions, various classes of methods have been developed to approximate the space of interest. The two classes that will be developed here are local approximations and basis representations. There are many additional methods that do not fit into these categories, but these two are sufficient for providing the context of how neural networks fit into the bigger picture of nonparametric modeling. Further references on nonparametric modeling are widely available, for example, Härdle (1990), Hastie, Tibshirani, and Friedman (2001), Duda, Hart, and Stork (2001), and Gentle (2002).

In this chapter, we will first examine a number of different nonparametric regression methods, with particular attention on those using a basis representation. Next will be a discussion of classification methods, which are often simple extensions of regression techniques. Within this framework, we will introduce neural network models, which will be shown to fit right in with the other basis representation methods. A brief review of the Bayesian paradigm follows, along with a discussion of how it relates to neural networks in particular. Finally, there will be a discussion of model building within the context of nonparametric modeling, which will also set the stage for the rest of the book.

11

2.1 Nonparametric Regression

The typical linear regression problem is to find a vector of coefficients β to maximize the likelihood of the model

$$y_i = \beta^t \mathbf{x}_i + \varepsilon_i \,, \tag{2.1}$$

where y_i is the ith case of the response variable, $\mathbf{x}_i = \{x_{i1}, \ldots, x_{ir}\}$ is the vector of corresponding values of the explanatory variables, and the residuals, ε_i, are *iid* Gaussian with mean zero and a common variance. The assumption of a straight line (or a hyperplane) fit may be overly restrictive. Even a family of transformations may be insufficiently flexible to fit many datasets. Instead, we may want a much richer class of possible response functions. The typical nonparametric regression model is of the form

$$y_i = f(\mathbf{x}_i) + \varepsilon_i \,, \tag{2.2}$$

where $f \in \mathcal{F}$, some class of regression functions, $\mathbf{x}_i$, is the vector of explanatory variables, and ε_i is *iid* additive error with mean zero and constant variance, usually assumed to have a Gaussian distribution (as we will here). The main distinction between the competing nonparametric methods is the class of functions, $\mathcal{F}$, to which f is assumed to belong. The common feature is that functions in $\mathcal{F}$ should be able to approximate a very large range of functions, such as the set of all continuous functions, or the set of all square-integrable functions. We will now look at a variety of different ways to choose $\mathcal{F}$, and hence a nonparametric regression model. This section focuses only on the two classes of methods that most closely relate to neural networks: local methods and basis representations. Note that it is not critical for the flow of this book for the reader to understand all of the details in this section; the variety of methods is provided as context for how neural networks fit into the statistical literature. Descriptions of the methods here are rather brief, with references provided for further information. While going through the methods in this chapter, the reader may find Figure 2.3 helpful in understanding the relationships between these methods.

2.1.1 Local Methods

Some of the simplest approaches to nonparametric regression are those which operate locally. In one dimension, a moving average with a fixed window size would be an obvious example that is both simple and local. With a fixed window, the moving average estimate is a step function. More sophisticated things can be done in terms of the choice of window, the weighting of the averaging, or the shape of the fit over the window, as demonstrated by the following methods.

The idea of kernel smoothing is to use a moving weighted average, where the weight function is referred to as a kernel. A kernel is a continuous, bounded, symmetric function whose integral is one. The simplest kernel would be the indicator function over the interval from $-\frac{1}{2}$ to $\frac{1}{2}$, i.e., $K(x) = I_{[-\frac{1}{2} \leq x \leq \frac{1}{2}]}$, resulting in a step function regression. Other choices of kernels may vary smoothly to zero on either side, including functions such as the Epanechnikov kernel, $K(x) = \frac{3}{4}(1 - x^2)I_{[-1 \leq x \leq 1]}$ (Epanechnikov (1969)), or the Gaussian kernel (the density function for a standard Gaussian distribution). Whatever the choice of kernel, the resulting regression function estimate at a value x of a single explanatory variable is

$$\hat{y} = \frac{\sum\limits_{i=1}^{n} y_i K(x - x_i)}{\sum\limits_{i=1}^{n} K(x - x_i)}.$$

The kernel regression approach is intertwined with work on kernel density estimation. More details on these topics are available in many books and articles, for example, Silverman (1986), Härdle (1991), and Loader (1999). Kernels can be generalized to multiple dimensions, but data sparseness quickly becomes an issue. One relevant generalization of a Gaussian kernel approach is Gaussian process regression, which defines a process over the whole space with the distribution of any finite set of points being a multivariate Gaussian. More details on Gaussian processes, including the choice of spatial correlation functions, can be found in Cressie (1991), for example. Bayesian adaptations exist (O'Hagan (1978); Hjort and Omre (1994); Williams and Rasmussen (1996); Neal (1999)), and connections have been drawn to neural network models (Neal (1996); Gibbs and MacKay (1997)).

In addition to using weights based on distance to the point, fits other than a weighted moving average can be used. For example, locally weighted scatterplot smoothing (LOWESS) (Cleveland (1979)) uses locally weighted polynomials. The original LOWESS algorithm also takes some additional measures to ensure that the fit is robust with respect to outliers.

A completely different approach is to abandon the moving window in favor of partitioning the space into an exhaustive set of mutually exclusive intervals (or regions). Using a constant function over the region gives rise to a step function. In one dimension, this is a histogram estimator (see, for example, Gentle (2002, Section 9.2)).

In higher dimensions, a tree is a useful method for representing the splitting of the space into regions. With a constant fit over each region, this method is known as recursive partitioning regression (RPR) or classification and regression trees (CART) (Breiman et al. (1984)). CART has become popular because of its ease of use, clear interpretation of results, and ability to fit reasonably well in many cases. Typically binary splits of covariates are used, and covariates may be revisited. For regression, the predicted value is the average value of the response variable of cases in a bin, and, for classification, the fitted probability of class membership is the empirical probability in that bin (the number of cases in the bin in that class divided by the total number of cases in that bin). A simple regression example is shown in Figure 2.1, which applies a tree model to the ozone data, predicting ozone levels from wind speed and humidity (ignoring the other possible covariates). The top graph is a dendrogram, which labels each split starting from the top, with the fitted values in the "leaves" at the bottom (e.g., if humidity is above 59.5% and wind speed is above 8.5 mph, then the predicted ozone concentration is 4.4 ppm). The bottom graph shows the recursive partitioning of the space of explanatory variables, with the first split indicated by the solid line, the two next levels of splits by dashed lines, and the one third-level split with a dotted line. The fitted ozone value is labeled for each partition and is merely the average ozone measurement of all cases in that partition. Tree models can be extended to allow the fitting of linear regression or other more complex models over each of the regions (Chipman, George,

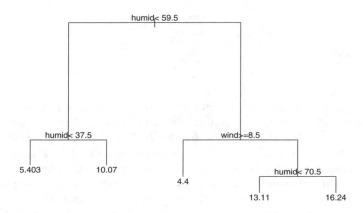

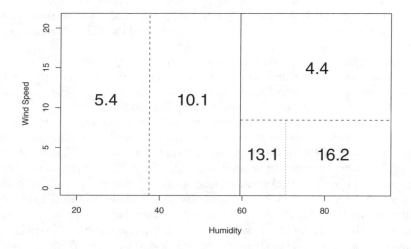

Figure 2.1. *A tree model for ozone using only wind speed and humidity. The top graph is a dendrogram of the fitted tree, and the bottom shows the bins of the explanatory variables with the fitted ozone values labeled for each bin.*

and McCulloch (2002)). Bayesian versions of CART have also been explored (Denison, Mallick, and Smith (1998a); Chipman, George, and McCulloch (1998)). Partition models can also be generalized beyond trees, such as with a Voronoi tesselation partition (Denison et al. (2002)).

Returning to a partition on a single dimension, spline smoothing uses low-order polynomials over the partition elements, with the maximum order specified as part of the model. The boundary points of the partitions are referred to as "knots," and it is required that the resulting spline fit be continuous at the knots. Furthermore, continuity of derivatives (often up to one less than the order of the polynomials used) is also mandated, thus ensuring smoothness of the fitted regression function. There are a variety of flavors of splines; more details are available in references such as de Boor (2002), Green and Silverman (1994), and Wahba (1990).

Splines have proven very useful in single-dimensional problems. Generalization to multiple dimensions is more problematic. The canonical idea is to use tensor products of unidimensional splines. While conceptually straightforward, there are many practical complications. Chui (1988) provides an in-depth discussion of multivariate splines. A special case is multivariate adaptive regression splines (MARS) (Friedman (1991)), which uses a "hockey stick" base function, $f_j(x_{ij}) = s_j(x_{ij} - t_j)_+$, where s is a sign function (either $+1$ or -1) and t is a threshold. This is a linear spline with a single knot at t_j, and it is set to zero on one side of the knot (depending on s). This is adapted to the multivariate setting by taking a tensor product of these linear splines, $f(\mathbf{x}_i) = \prod_j f_j(x_{ij})$. Denison, Mallick, and Smith describe a Bayesian version of MARS (1998b). An alternative to tensor products is simple linear combinations, i.e., $f(\mathbf{x}_i) = \sum_j \beta_j (\boldsymbol{\gamma}^t \mathbf{x}_i)_+ + \varepsilon_i$, where $\boldsymbol{\gamma}$ are the coefficients for the "hyperplane spline" and $(z)_+ = \max(0, z)$ (Friedman and Stuetzle (1981); Holmes and Mallick (2001)).

A multivariate extension to splines that is simpler to use in practice is the generalized additive model (GAM) (Hastie and Tibshirani (1990)). A separate spline fit is used for each explanatory variable so that only univariate splines are necessary. They are fit simultaneously as to give an additive model:

$$y_i = \sum_{j=1}^{r} f_j(x_{ij}) + \varepsilon_i \,,$$

where each f_j is a one-dimensional spline. Such models are fairly flexible and computationally tractable. Returning to the introduction of the ozone data in the first chapter, Figure 1.2 shows the nine f_j components of a GAM fit for ozone concentration from the covariates. For example, from the upper left plot we see that fitted ozone increases approximately linearly with VH (the altitude at which the pressure is 500 millibars), while the lower right plot shows that fitted ozone is highest in the spring and early summer. The effect of each covariate is independent of the others, since the model is additive.

A further generalization of GAM is projection pursuit regression (PPR), which recognizes that additivity on the original coordinate axes may be insufficient but that some rotation of the axes may provide a much better fit (Friedman and Stuetzle (1981)). Thus it uses linear combinations of the explanatory variables (a "pursued direction") as the new inputs to the additive splines:

$$y_i = \sum_{j=1}^{r} f_j(\boldsymbol{\beta}^t \mathbf{x}_i) + \varepsilon_i \,, \tag{2.3}$$

where the f_j are univariate splines. The conceptual idea is that the f_j are fully flexible, and so PPR is fitting a linear combination of arbitrary smooth functions on a new coordinate system chosen to best describe the data. In this sense, we will see that a neural network can be viewed as a special case of PPR, where the functional form of f_j is restricted to scaled logistic functions (cf. equation (2.6)).

2.1.2   Regression Using Basis Functions

A large class of nonparametric methods are those that use an infinite set of basis functions to span the space of interest, typically either the space of continuous functions or the space of square-integrable functions. This overview begins with some of the more obvious examples, building to more complex cases. In Section 2.3, we will see that neural networks also fit into this category. The key concept is that the regression model is of the form

$$y_i = \sum_{j=0}^{k} \beta_j f_j(\mathbf{x}_i) + \varepsilon_i , \tag{2.4}$$

where $f_1, f_2, \ldots$ is a set of basis functions. Typically f_0 is defined to be 1 everywhere, providing the constant term. Since an infinite number of terms would typically be required for a theoretical match to a continuous function, this approach could be thought of as "infinitely parametric," rather than "nonparametric," but the latter term is commonly used. In practice, a finite number of terms (and parameters) provides a close approximation to the infinite sum.

A simple example of a basis set that spans the space of continuous functions in one dimension is the set of basic polynomial functions, $\{1, x, x^2, x^3, x^4, \ldots\}$, i.e., $f_j(x) = x^j$. Any continuous function can be approximated arbitrarily closely with a linear combination of these functions, provided a large enough number of them are used (with more needed for less smooth functions). In practice, it is often preferred that the basis set consist of orthogonal elements, so many classes of orthogonal polynomials have been developed, including Legendre, Laguerre, Hermite, Chebyshev, Jacobi, and ultraspherical (Abramowitz and Stegun (1965)).

Another well-known example of a basis set representation is Fourier series regression. By taking a sufficiently large number of sine and cosine functions of different frequencies and amplitudes, one can approximate any square-integrable function as well as desired. This basis set also has the advantage of orthogonality. If the underlying function is periodic, the coefficients will have meaningful interpretations, but if the function is aperiodic, it is difficult to have any intuition for the coefficients, a problem shared by many basis function methods, including neural networks as we shall see in Chapter 3. It should be noted that it is not trivial to adapt either polynomial or trigonometric basis functions to a multidimensional setting.

Mixture models can be basis representations, depending on the particular form of the model. One common form of mixtures, particularly for density estimation but also for regression, is a mixture of normals. A collection of Gaussian densities is used as a basis set. For a univariate problem, the model is

$$y_i = \beta_0 + \sum_{j=1}^{k} \beta_j \phi \left(\frac{x_i - \mu_j}{\sigma_j} \right) + \varepsilon_i , \tag{2.5}$$

where $\phi(x) = \frac{1}{\sqrt{2\pi}} \exp\{-x^2/2\}$ is the standard Gaussian density function. For multivariate **x**, a distance $||x_i - \mu_j||$, usually Euclidean, replaces the difference $x_i - \mu_j$. Within the context of machine learning, when all the σ_j are equal, this model is referred to as a *radial basis network*. Many of the issues addressed in this book are more straightforward for radial basis networks where good solutions exist (Holmes and Mallick (1998); Andrieu, de Freitas, and Doucet (2001)).

Wavelets have gained much popularity, particularly for signal processing but also for nonparametric regression in general. They also work by creating a set of basis functions. They take a starting function, $\phi(x)$ (which in the wavelet literature is a generic function, not necessarily the standard Gaussian density), called the "mother wavelet," and then use a scaling function to get the whole basis set. For example, the Haar function can be written $\phi(x) = I_{[0,\frac{1}{2})}(x) - I_{[\frac{1}{2},1)}(x)$. The rest of the bases are integer location-scale versions, $\phi_{j,k}(x) = 2^{j/2}\phi(2^j x - k)$. This produces an (infinite) orthogonal basis set. Figure 2.2 shows the Haar mother wavelet (solid line) and two more members of the family (with $j = 1, 2$ and $k = 0$). There are many other widely used choices of mother wavelets and associated scaling functions, some of which produce orthogonal basis sets and some of which do not (Ogden (1997); Vidakovic (1999)). Wavelet networks and Bayesian wavelet networks can also be applied to nonparametric regression (Holmes and Mallick (2000)).

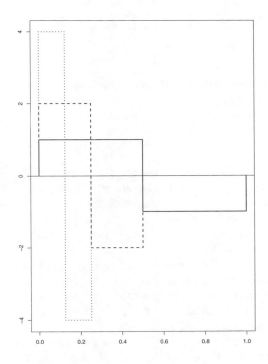

Figure 2.2. *Example wavelets from the Haar family.*

Local Methods   Basis Function Methods

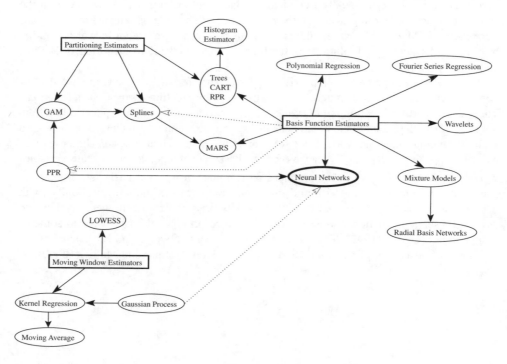

Figure 2.3. *Diagram of nonparametric methods: Local methods are on the left, and basis methods are on the right; special cases are represented by a solid line with a → b meaning that b is a special case of a; the dashed lines represent approximations and limiting cases.*

While both CART and MARS are usually presented as part of the family of local approximation methods, they can also be thought of as basis representations. One of the basic tools used in real analysis is the fact that the class of step functions can approximate any continuous function. Thus CART can be seen as using step functions as a basis set for approximating smooth functions. For MARS, the basis set is comprised of the hockey stick functions and their tensor products.

Indeed the whole idea of spline fitting is to use the fact that polynomials span the space of continuous functions. By partitioning the space, one can usually get by with very low order polynomials, instead of requiring a large number of terms (as well as eliminating wild oscillations beyond the boundaries of the data). Thus splines, as well as PPR, can be seen as approximate basis representation methods.

To summarize this overview of nonparametric regression techniques in the classes that relate to neural networks, Figure 2.3 shows the local methods on the left and the basis representation methods on the right. Lines connect related methods. A solid line from one method to another shows that the second method is a special case of the first (e.g., a histogram estimator is a special case of a tree estimator). Dashed lines indicate approximations (PPR and splines are approximations to basis representations) and limiting relationships (a limiting case of a neural network can be a special case of a Gaussian process). The relations involving neural networks are described in Section 2.3.1.

2.2 Nonparametric Classification

The goal of classification is to provide a model for sorting observations into predetermined categories. The number of categories is fixed in advance. Observed data are used to create a model that can then predict category membership for other possible values of the explanatory variables. Most methods actually model the probability that an observation belongs to a particular category as a function of its explanatory variables, and a categorical prediction can be obtained by selecting the category with highest fitted probability. Some methods (such as single-nearest neighbor) give only a categorical prediction, without estimated probabilities.

Many nonparametric methods for classification are closely related to regression methods. In this section we will look at two major groups of these methods, in order to give a context for classification using neural networks. There are many other methods for classification, and the reader is referred to other references for additional methods or details (Hastie, Tibshirani, and Friedman (2001); Duda, Hart, and Stork (2001); Gordon (1999); Denison et al. (2002)).

Many regression techniques can be turned into classification methods by applying them to the problem of density estimation for the category probabilities. For example, if there are only two categories, denote them by $Y \in \{0, 1\}$. The regression problem is to model $E[Y|X]$, and now this can be applied directly to categorical Y, since, for $Y \in \{0, 1\}$, $P(Y = 1|X) = E[Y|X]$. Thus any of the above regression methods can be directly applied to classification. For a categorical response with more than two categories, a multivariate response regression can be used with a response vector consisting of indicator variables for the different categories. One major drawback of this approach is that direct application of regression techniques will not guarantee that the fitted function takes values only between zero and one, as would be required of a probability. In practice, a transformation of the fitted response (regression) is typically used to convert a response along the real line to a response in the interval [0, 1], such as the logistic function $\Psi(z) = \frac{1}{1+\exp(-z)}$ or the normal cdf $\Psi(z) = \int_{-\infty}^{z} \frac{1}{\sqrt{2\pi}} \exp\{-z^2/2\} dz$. Neural networks are used this way, as discussed in detail in Section 2.3.4.

Another major class of classification techniques that directly relates to their use in regression is the set of partition methods. Methods such as decision trees (including CART) can be used to divide the space into nonoverlapping sets, and fitted probabilities of class membership are assigned to each set, based on the observed counts within that set. Nearest neighbor methods are the classification analogue of moving window regression. For k-nearest neighbor classification, the user specifies a parameter k, the number of neighbors being used (and hence the relative size of the window). The fitted class membership function at any point in the space of the explanatory variables is defined as the class that comprises the majority (or plurality, if there are more than two classes) of the observed classes of the k closest observed data points (nearest neighbors) in the space of explanatory variables.

Thus the space is partitioned by a moving window of majority votes. The nearest neighbor algorithm can also be adapted to be probabilistic and Bayesian (Holmes and Adams (2002)).

2.3   Neural Networks

Here we introduce neural network models within the context of nonparametric regression. Deeper understanding of the model and its parameters, as well as a detailed example, will be deferred to Chapter 3. In this book, we will focus on neural network models for regression with the following form:

$$y_i = \beta_0 + \sum_{j=1}^{k} \beta_j \Psi(\boldsymbol{\gamma}_j^t \mathbf{x}_i) + \varepsilon_i \,, \tag{2.6}$$

where k is the number of basis functions (hidden nodes), the β_j's are the weights of the basis functions, the γ_j's are vectors of location and scale parameters (with elements γ_{jh}, where h indexes over covariates), $\varepsilon_i \overset{iid}{\sim} N(0, \sigma^2)$ is the error term, and Ψ is the logistic function:

$$\Psi(z) = \frac{1}{1 + \exp(-z)} \,. \tag{2.7}$$

In words, a neural network is usually described in terms of its "hidden nodes." Each hidden node can be thought of as a function, taking a linear combination of the explanatory variables ($\boldsymbol{\gamma}_j^t \mathbf{x}_i$) as an input and returning the logistic transformation (equation (2.7)) as its output. The neural network then takes a linear combination of the outputs of the hidden nodes to give the fitted value at a point. Figure 2.4 shows this process pictorially. (Note that this diagram is an expanded version of Figure 1.5.) Combining equations (2.6) and (2.7) and

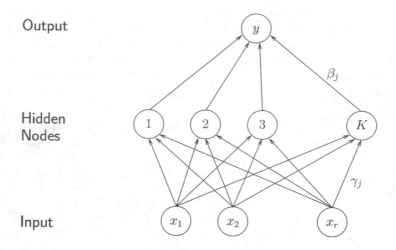

Figure 2.4. *Neural network model diagram.*

expanding the vector notation yields the following equation, which shows the model in its full glory (or goriness):

$$y_i = \beta_0 + \sum_{j=1}^{k} \beta_j \frac{1}{1 + \exp\left(-\gamma_{j0} - \sum_{h=1}^{r} \gamma_{jh} x_{ih}\right)} + \varepsilon_i \,,$$

where k is the number of basis functions and r is the number of explanatory variables. The parameters of this model are k (the number of hidden nodes), β_j for $j \in \{0, \dots, k\}$, and γ_{jh} for $j \in \{1, \dots, k\}$, $h \in \{0, \dots, r\}$. For a fixed network size (fixed k), the number of parameters, d, is

$$d = (r + 1) * k + (k + 1) = k * (r + 2) + 1 \,, \qquad (2.8)$$

where the first term in the sum is the number of γ_{jh} and the second is the number of β_j.

It is clear from equation (2.6) that a neural network is simply a nonparametric regression using a basis representation (compare to equation (2.4)), with the Ψ_j's, location-scale logistic functions, as the bases and the β_j's as their coefficients. The (infinite) set of location-scale logistic functions does span the space of continuous functions, as well as the space of square-integrable functions (Cybenko (1989); Funahashi (1989); Hornik, Stinchcombe, and White (1989)). While these bases are not orthogonal, they have turned out to be quite useful in practice, with a relatively small number able to approximate a wide range of functions.

The key to understanding a neural network model is to think of it in terms of basis functions. Interpretation of the individual parameters will be deferred to Chapter 3. For now, we note that if we use a single basis function (hidden node) and restrict $\beta_0 = 0$ and $\beta_1 = 1$, then this simple neural network is exactly the same as a standard logistic regression model. Thus a neural network can be interpreted as a linear combination of logistic regressions.

2.3.1   Neural Networks Are Statistical Models

From equation (2.6), it is obvious that a neural network is a standard parametric model, with a likelihood and parameters to be fit. When compared to the models in Section 2.1.2, one can see how neural networks are just another example of a basis function method for nonparametric regression (classification will similarly be discussed shortly). While the form of equation (2.6) may not be the most intuitive expression in the world, it is a special case of equations (2.2) and (2.4) and is clearly a model. It is not magic, and it is only a black box if the user wants to pretend they have never looked at equation (2.6). While some people have claimed that neural networks are purely algorithms and not models, it should now be apparent that they are both algorithms and models.

By viewing neural networks as statistical models, we can now apply many other ideas in statistics in order to understand, improve, and appropriately use these models. The disadvantage of viewing them as algorithms is that it can be difficult to apply knowledge from other algorithms. Taking the model-based perspective, we can be more systematic in discussing issues such as choosing a prior, building a model, checking assumptions for the validity of the model, and understanding uncertainty in our predictions.

It is also worth noting that a neural network can be viewed as a special case of projection pursuit regression (equation (2.3)) where the arbitrary smooth functions are restricted to scaled logistic functions. Furthermore, in the limit with an arbitrarily large number of basis functions, a neural network can be made to converge to a Gaussian process model (Neal (1996)).

2.3.2   A Brief History of Neural Networks

While neural networks are statistical models, they have mostly been developed from the algorithmic perspective of machine learning. Neural networks were originally created as an attempt to model the act of thinking by modeling neurons in a brain. Much of the early work in this area traces back to a paper by McCulloch and Pitts (1943) which introduced the idea of an activation function, although the authors used a threshold (indicator) function rather than the sigmoidal functions common today (an S-shaped function that has horizontal asymptotes in both directions from its center and rises smoothly and monotonically between its asymptotes, e.g., equation (2.7)). This particular model did not turn out to be appropriate for modeling brains but did eventually lead to useful statistical models. Modern neural networks are sometimes referred to as *artificial neural networks* to emphasize that there is no longer any explicit connection to biology.

Early networks of threshold function nodes were explored by Rosenblatt (1962) (calling them perceptrons, a term that is sometimes still used for nodes) and Widrow and Hoff (1960) (calling them adalines). Threshold activations were found to have severe limitations (Minsky and Papert (1969)), and thus sigmoidal activations became widely used instead (Anderson (1982)).

Much of the recent work on neural networks stems from renewed interest generated by Rumelhart, Hinton, and Williams (1986) and their backpropagation algorithm for fitting the parameters of the network. A number of key papers followed, including Funahashi (1989), Cybenko (1989), and Hornik, Stinchcombe, and White (1989), that showed that neural networks are a way to approximate a function arbitrarily closely as the number of hidden nodes gets large. Mathematically, they have shown that the infinite set of location-scale logistic functions is indeed a basis set for many common spaces, such as the space of continuous functions, or square-integrable functions.

2.3.3   Multivariate Regression

To extend the above model to a multivariate $\mathbf{y}$, we simply treat each dimension of $\mathbf{y}$ as a separate output and add a set of connections from each hidden node to each of the dimensions of $\mathbf{y}$. In this implementation, we assume that the error variance is the same for all dimensions, although this would be easily generalized to separate variances for each component. Denote the vector of the ith observation as $\mathbf{y}_i$ so that the gth component (dimension) of $\mathbf{y}_i$ is denoted y_{ig}. The model is now

$$y_{ig} = \beta_{0g} + \sum_{j=1}^{k} \beta_{jg} \frac{1}{1 + \exp\left(-\gamma_{j0} - \sum_{h=1}^{r} \gamma_{jh} x_{ih}\right)} + \varepsilon_{ig}, \tag{2.9}$$

$$\varepsilon_{ig} \overset{iid}{\sim} N(0, \sigma^2). \tag{2.10}$$

Thus each dimension of the output is modeled as a different linear combination of the same basis functions. This is displayed pictorially in Figure 2.5.

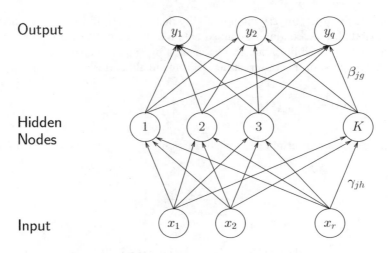

Figure 2.5. *Multivariate response neural network model diagram.*

2.3.4   Classification

The multivariate response model is easily extended to the problem of classification. There are several possible approaches, two of which will be discussed here. The first is the more common approach of transforming the output to the probability scale, leading to a standard multinomial likelihood. The second approach uses latent variables, retaining a Gaussian likelihood of sorts, leaving it much closer to the regression model.

For the multinomial likelihood approach, the key to extending this model to classification is to express the categorical response variable as a vector of indicator (dummy) variables. A multivariate neural network is then fit to this vector of indicator variables with the outputs transformed to a probability scale so that the multinomial likelihood can be used. Let t_i be the categorical response (the *target*) with its value being the category number to which case i belongs, $t_i \in \{1, \ldots, q\}$, where q is the number of categories. Note that the ordering of the categories does not matter in this formulation. Let $\mathbf{y}_i$ be a vector in the alternate representation of the response (a vector of indicator variables), where $y_{ig} = 1$ when $g = y_i$ and zero otherwise.

For example, suppose we are trying to classify tissue samples into the categories "benign tumor," "malignant tumor," and "no tumor," and our observed dataset (the training set) is {benign, none, malignant, benign, malignant}. We have three categories, so $q = 3$ and we get the following recoding:

$$
\begin{array}{lll}
y_{11} = 1 & y_{12} = 0 & y_{13} = 0 \\
y_{21} = 0 & y_{22} = 0 & y_{23} = 1 \\
y_{31} = 0 & y_{32} = 1 & y_{33} = 0 \\
y_{41} = 1 & y_{42} = 0 & y_{43} = 0 \\
y_{51} = 0 & y_{52} = 1 & y_{53} = 0 \, .
\end{array}
$$

Let p_{ig} be the (true) underlying probability that $y_{ig} = 1$. To use a neural network to fit these probabilities, the continuous-valued output of the neural network (denoted w_{ig}) is transformed to the probability scale by exponentiating and normalizing by the sum of all exponentiated outputs for that observation. Thus the likelihood is

$$f\left(\mathbf{y}|\mathbf{p}\right) = \prod_{i=1}^{n} f\left(t_i | p_{i1}, \dots, p_{iq}\right) \propto \prod_{i=1}^{n} \left(p_{i1}\right)^{(y_{i1})} \cdots \left(p_{iq}\right)^{(y_{iq})} . \qquad (2.11)$$

The parameters p_{ig} are deterministic transformations of the neural network parameters $\boldsymbol{\beta}$ and $\boldsymbol{\gamma}$:

$$p_{ig} = \frac{\exp\left(w_{ig}\right)}{\sum_{h=1}^{q} \exp\left(w_{ih}\right)} ,$$

$$w_{ig} = \beta_{0g} + \sum_{j=1}^{k} \beta_{jg} \Psi_j(\boldsymbol{\gamma}_j^t \mathbf{x}_i) , \text{ and}$$

$$\Psi_j(\boldsymbol{\gamma}_j^t \mathbf{x}_i) = \frac{1}{1 + \exp\left(-\gamma_{j0} - \sum_{h=1}^{r} \gamma_{jh} x_{ih}\right)} ,$$

where $i = 1, \dots, n$ represents the different cases, $j = 1, \dots, k$ are the different hidden nodes (logistic basis functions), and $g = 1, \dots, q$ are the different classes being predicted. Note that in practice, only the first $q - 1$ elements of y are used in fitting the neural network so that the problem is of full rank. The w_{iq} term is set to zero (for all i) for identifiability of the model.

For a fixed network size (fixed k), the number of parameters, d, is

$$d = (r + 1) * k + (k + 1) * (q - 1) = k * (q + r) + q - 1 , \qquad (2.12)$$

where the first term in the sum is the number of γ_{jh} and the second is the number of β_{jg}.

This model is referred to as the *softmax* model in the field of computer science (Bridle (1989)). This method of reparameterizing the probabilities from a continuous scale can be found in other areas of statistics as well, such as generalized linear regression (McCullagh and Nelder (1989, p. 159)) .

As an alternative to the multinomial likelihood, one can use a latent variable approach to modify the original model to directly do classification, retaining an underlying Gaussian likelihood, and thus retaining the properties of the original network (as well as being able to more readily reuse computer code).

Again, we code the categories numerically so that the ith observation is in category t_i, and we construct indicator variables for each of the q possible categories. Again, we run the neural network for the indicator variables and denote the continuous-valued outputs (predictions of the latent variables) by w_{ig}. Now instead of using a multinomial distribution for t_i, we deterministically set the fitted value $\hat{t}_i$ to be

$$\hat{t}_i = \underset{g \in \{1, \dots, q\}}{\operatorname{argmax}} w_{ig};$$

i.e., the fitted response is the category with the largest w_{ig}. Note that we set $w_{iq} = 0$ for all i, in order to ensure the model is well specified (otherwise the location of all of the w_{ig}'s could be shifted by a constant without changing the model). Thus this model preserves the original regression likelihood but now applies it to latent variables, with the latent variables producing a deterministic fitted value on the categorical scale.

This approach also has the advantage of a simple extension to ordinal response variables, those which have a clear ordering but are categorical, where the differences between categories cannot be directly converted to distances, so treating them as continuous is not realistic. For example, a survey may offer the responses of "excellent," "good," "fair," and "poor," which are certainly ordered but with no natural distance metric between levels. To fit an ordinal variable, we again let t_i code the category of the ith observation, but this time the ordering of the categories is important. We no longer need the indicator variables, and instead we just fit a single neural network and denote its continuous output by w_i. We then convert this output to a category by dividing the real line into bins and matching the bins to the ordered categories. To be precise, we have additional parameters $c_1, \ldots, c_{q-1}$, with $c_g < c_{g+1}$, that are the cut-off values for the bins. Thus if $c_{h-1} < w_i \leq c_h$, then we predict observation i to be in category h, i.e., $\hat{t}_i = h$. For example, if $c_1 < w_6 \leq c_2$, then the sixth observation is assigned to the second category. If $w_i < c_1$, then it is in category 1, and if $w_i > c_{q-1}$, then it is in category q. It is useful to fix $c_1 = 0$ so that the model is well specified. Note that if one conditions on an observation belonging to a particular category, w_i is a truncated normal.

For a classification example, we turn to the loan application dataset introduced in Section 1.4. To keep things simple, consider only the age variable in attempting to predict whether a loan was approved or not and estimating the probability of approval. Here we use the standard multinomial likelihood of equation (2.11). A neural network model with six basis functions was fit, and the probability of approval versus age is shown in Figure 2.6. Points denoted with an "x" are applications that were actually approved, and those marked "O" were declined. For display clarity, a sample of only 250 points is used in the plot (all the data are used in fitting the model) so that the symbols are visible in the plot. To get a prediction of class (approved or declined), one simply classifies those with probability at least .5 as approved and those with probability under .5 as declined. In general, older applicants are more likely to have their applications approved, but the fitted curve is not monotonic. While this nonmonotonicity improves the fit, it would not be a legally allowed model for the bank to use, because it is not legal to discriminate against older people in making loan decisions in the United States, and so giving people in their early fifties a lower probability of acceptance than people in their late forties would be an issue.

If a neural network with only four basis functions is used instead, the nonmonotonicity problem goes away. Figure 2.7 shows the fitted probabilities from this model. Probability of acceptance now increases smoothly and monotonically with age, resulting in a legal model. This model also fits almost as well, misclassifying only four more cases than the six basis function model. In many cases, there are statistical gains to be made from using a simpler model. In this case, there is also a legal gain. Statistical issues of choosing the number of basis functions will be addressed in Chapter 4.

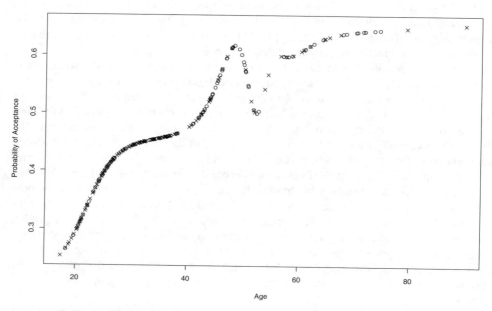

Figure 2.6. *Predicted probability of loan acceptance from a 6-node network using only the age of the applicant. An "x" marks a loan that was actually approved and an "O" a loan that was actually denied.*

2.3.5 Other Flavors of Neural Networks

The exact form of neural network model presented above (equation (2.6)) is referred to as a single hidden layer feed-forward neural network with logistic activation functions and a linear output. As one might expect from all of the terms in that description, there are a large number of variations possible. We shall discuss these briefly, and then we will return to the above basic model for the rest of this book.

The first term is "single hidden layer" which means there is just one set of "hidden nodes," the logistic basis functions, which are pictured as the middle row in Figure 2.4. With one set of hidden nodes, we have the straightforward basis representation interpretation. It is quite possible to add additional layers of hidden nodes, where each hidden node takes a linear combination of the outputs from the previous layer and produces its own output which is a logistic transformation of its input linear combination. The outputs of each layer are taken as the inputs of the next layer. As was proved by several groups, a single layer is all that is necessary to span most spaces of interest, so there is no additional flexibility to be gained by using multiple layers (Cybenko (1989); Funahashi (1989); Hornik, Stinchcombe, and White (1989)). However, sometimes adding layers will give a more compact representation, whereby a complex function can be approximated by a smaller total number of nodes in multiple layers than the number of nodes necessary if only a single layer is used.

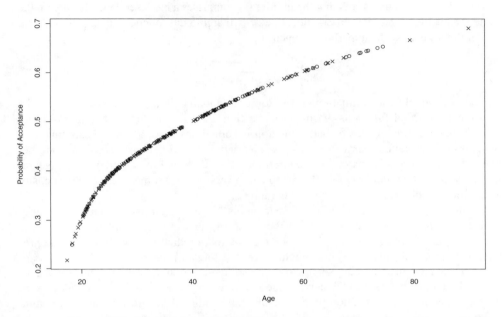

Figure 2.7. *Predicted probability of loan acceptance from a 4-node network using only the age of the applicant. An "x" marks a loan that was actually approved and an "O" a loan that was actually denied.*

A feed-forward network is one that has a distinct ordering to its layers so that the inputs to each layer are linear combinations of the outputs of the previous layer, as in Figure 2.4. Sometimes additional connections are made, connecting nonadjacent layers. For example, starting with our standard model, the third layer (the output prediction) could take as inputs a linear combination of both the hidden nodes (the second layer) and the explanatory variables (the first layer), which would give a model of the form

$$ y_i = \beta_0 + \boldsymbol{\alpha}^t \mathbf{x}_i + \sum_{j=1}^{k} \beta_j \Psi(\boldsymbol{\gamma}_j^t \mathbf{x}_i) \varepsilon_i \,, $$

which is often called a semiparametric model, because it contains both a parametric component (a standard linear regression, $\boldsymbol{\alpha}^t \mathbf{x}_i$) and a "nonparametric" component (the linear combination of location-scale logistic bases). Significantly more complex models can be made by allowing connections to go down layers as well, creating cycles in the graph of Figure 2.4. For example, suppose there are four total levels, with two layers of hidden nodes, the inputs of the second row of hidden nodes are linear combinations of the first row of hidden nodes as usual, but the inputs of the first row of hidden nodes include both the explanatory variables as well as the outputs from the second row of hidden nodes, thus creating a cycle. Such networks require iterative solutions and substantially more computing time, and are not as commonly used.

Logistic basis functions are the most commonly used. In theory, any sigmoidal function can be used, as the proofs that the infinite set comprises a basis set depends only on the functions being sigmoidal. In practice, one of two sigmoidal functions is usually chosen, either the logistic or the hyperbolic tangent:

$$\Psi'(z) = \frac{e^x - e^{-x}}{e^x + e^{-x}},$$

which is a simple transformation of the logistic function, $\Psi'(z) = 2\Psi(2z) - 1$. The historical threshold functions discussed in Section 2.3.2 are no longer commonly used. A completely different type of basis function is sometimes used, a *radial* basis function, which is usually called a kernel in statistics. Thus a radial basis network is basically another name for what statisticians call a mixture model, as described in equation (2.5). Neural network models, particularly radial basis function versions, are sometimes used for density estimation problems (see, for example, Bishop (1995)).

In our basic model, we use a "linear output" in that the final prediction is simply a linear combination of the outputs of the hidden layer. In other implementations, the logistic transformation may also be applied to the final prediction as well, producing predictions in the unit interval (which could be rescaled again if necessary). There does not seem to be any substantial advantage to doing so in a regression problem (but it is sometimes done nonetheless). Obviously, if one is fitting values restricted to an interval (e.g., probabilities for a classification problem), such an additional transformation can be quite useful.

2.4   The Bayesian Paradigm

The two main philosophies of probability and statistics are the *classical* and *Bayesian* approaches. While they share much in common, they have a fundamental difference in how they interpret probabilities and on the nature of unknown parameters. In the classical (or frequentist) framework, probabilities are typically interpreted as long-run relative frequencies. Unknown parameters are thought of as fixed quantities, so that there is a "right answer," even if we will never know what it is. The data are used to find a "best guess" for the values of the unknown parameters.

Under the Bayesian framework, probabilities are seen as inherently subjective so that, for each person, their probability statements reflect their personal beliefs about the relative likeliness of the possible outcomes. Unknown parameters are considered to be random so that they also have probability distributions. Instead of finding a single best guess for the unknown parameters, the usual approach is to estimate the distribution of the parameters using Bayes' theorem. First, a prior distribution must be specified, and this distribution is meant to reflect the subject's personal beliefs about the parameters, before the data are observed. In some cases, the prior will be constructed from previous experiments. This approach provides a mathematically coherent method for combining information from different sources. In other cases, the practitioner may either not know anything about the parameters or may want to use a prior that would be generally acceptable to many other people, rather than a personal one. Such priors are discussed further in Section 3.3. Once the prior, $P(\theta)$, is specified for the parameters, θ, Bayes' theorem combines the prior with the likelihood, $f(\mathbf{X}|\boldsymbol{\theta})$, to get the posterior:

$$P(\boldsymbol{\theta}|\mathbf{X}) = \frac{f(\mathbf{X}|\boldsymbol{\theta})P(\boldsymbol{\theta})}{P(\mathbf{X})} \ .$$

One useful type of prior is a *conjugate* prior, one that when combined with the likelihood produces a posterior in the same family. For example, if the likelihood specifies that $y_1, \ldots, y_n \overset{iid}{\sim} N(\mu, 1)$, then using a normal prior for μ, $\mu \sim N(a, 1)$ for some constant a, is a conjugate choice, because the posterior for μ will also be normal, in particular, $N(\frac{a+\sum y_i}{n+1}, \frac{1}{n+1})$. Note that the idea of conjugacy is likelihood dependent, in that a prior is conjugate for a particular likelihood. Conjugate priors are widely used for convenience, as they lead to analytically tractable posteriors. In many cases, such as a neural network, there is no known conjugate prior. Instead, priors for individual parameters may be chosen to be *conditionally conjugate*, in that when all other parameters are conditioned upon (held fixed), the conditional posterior is of the same family as the conditional prior. For example, in Chapter 3, nearly all of the priors presented for neural networks will put a normal distribution on the β_j parameters (possibly conditioned upon the other parameters), which is conditionally conjugate. The main benefit of conditional conjugacy is that it allows one to use Gibbs sampling, as will be described in section 3.5, which greatly helps in model fitting.

This book will assume that the reader has some previous knowledge of the Bayesian approach. For more details on the Bayesian approach, as well as for discussion of the philosophical merits and criticisms of the Bayesian approach, the reader is referred to some of the many other sources available (Robert (2001); Congdon (2001); Carlin and Louis (2000); Gelman et al. (1995); Bernardo and Smith (1994); Press (1989); Hartigan (1983); Jeffreys (1961)).

The approach in this book will be the Bayesian one. However, it is more of a pragmatic Bayesian approach, rather than a dogmatic subjectivist approach. As we shall see in Section 3.1, in most cases the parameters do not have straightforward interpretations, and thus it is not feasible to put subjective knowledge into a prior. In the event that the data analyst has substantive prior information, a model with more interpretable parameters should be used instead of a neural network. If something is known about the shape of the data, another more accessible model should be chosen. The strength of neural networks is their flexibility, as was described in Section 2.3. A key benefit of the Bayesian approach is a full accounting of uncertainty. By estimating a posterior distribution, one obtains estimates of error and uncertainty in the process. Such uncertainty can also encompass the choice of model, as will be discussed in the next section.

2.5 Model Building

A full analysis of any data set involves many steps, starting with exploratory data analysis and moving on to formal model building. The process of choosing a model is typically an iterative one. Outside of the simplest problems, it is quite rare for the first model specified to be the final model. First, one must check the validity of the assumptions. Then one should see if the data suggest that a different model may be more appropriate. For example, when fitting a multiple linear regression, it is important to check that the residuals do follow the assumptions, and, if not, then usually a transformation is performed on the data to improve the situation. Also important is to check that the right set of variables has been included in the model. Variables which are found to be irrelevant or redundant are removed. Variables which were not initially included but are later found to be helpful would be added. Thus a series of models will be investigated before settling upon a final model or set of models.

The same procedure applies to modeling via neural networks. It is important to check the key assumptions of the model. Residual plots should be made to verify normality, independence, and constant variance (homoscedasticity). Violations of any assumption calls for a remedy, typically a transformation of one or more variables. Many of the guidelines for linear regression are applicable here as well.

Also important is the issue of model selection (or some alternative, such as model averaging; see Section 4.1). There are two parts to this issue when dealing with neural networks: choosing the set of explanatory variables and choosing the number of hidden nodes. (An additional complication could be choosing the network structure, if one considers networks beyond just single hidden layer feed-forward neural networks with logistic activation functions and a linear output, but that is beyond the scope of this book.)

First consider choosing an optimal set of explanatory variables. For a given dataset, using more explanatory variables will improve the fit. However, if the variables are not actually relevant, they will not help with prediction. Consider the mean square error for predictions, which has two components—the square of the prediction bias (expected misprediction) and the prediction variance. The use of irrelevant variables will have no effect on the prediction bias but will increase the prediction variance. Inclusion of unique relevant variables will reduce both bias and variance. Inclusion of redundant (e.g., correlated) variables will not change the prediction bias but will increase the variance. Thus the goal is to find all of the nonredundant useful explanatory variables, removing all variables which do not improve prediction.

The second aspect is selecting the optimal number of hidden nodes (or basis functions). Using more nodes allows a more complex fitted function. Fewer nodes lead to a smoother function. For a particular dataset, the more nodes used, the better the fit. With enough hidden nodes, the function can fit the data perfectly, becoming an interpolating function. However, such a function will usually perform poorly at prediction, as it fluctuates wildly in attempting to model the noise in the data in addition to the underlying trend. Just as with any other nonparametric procedure, an optimal amount of smoothing must be found so that the fitted function is neither overfitting (not smooth enough) or underfitting (too smooth).

Both of these aspects of model selection will be discussed in Chapter 4. That chapter will investigate criteria for selection, as well as methods for searching through the space of possible models. It will also discuss some alternatives to the traditional approach of choosing only a single model.

Chapter 3

Priors for Neural Networks

One of the key decisions in a Bayesian analysis is the choice of prior. The idea is that one's prior should reflect one's current beliefs (either from previous data or from purely subjective sources) about the parameters before one has observed the data. This task turns out to be rather difficult for a neural network, because in most cases the parameters have no interpretable meaning, merely being coefficients in a nonstandard basis expansion (as described in Section 2.3). In certain special cases, the parameters do have intuitive meanings, as will be discussed in the next section. In general, however, the parameters are basically uninterpretable, and thus the idea of putting beliefs into one's prior is rather quixotic. The next two sections discuss several practical choices of priors. This is followed by a practical discussion of parameter estimation, a comparison of some of the priors in this chapter, and some theoretical results on asymptotic consistency.

3.1   Parameter Interpretation, and Lack Thereof

In some specific cases, the parameters of a neural network have obvious interpretations. We will first look at these cases, and then a simple example will show how things can quickly go wrong and become virtually uninterpretable.

The first case is that of a neural network with only one hidden node and one explanatory variable. The model for the fitted values is

$$\hat{y}_i = \beta_0 + \frac{\beta_1}{1 + \exp(-\gamma_0 - \gamma_1 x_i)} \, .$$

Figure 3.1 shows this fitted function for $\beta_0 = -2$, $\beta_1 = 4$, $\gamma_0 = -9$, and $\gamma_1 = 15$ over x in the unit interval. The parameter β_0 is an overall location parameter for y, in that $y = \beta_0$ when the logistic function is close to zero (in this case when x is near or below zero, so here β_0 is the y-intercept). The parameter β_1 is an overall scale factor for y, in that the logistic function ranges from 0 to 1 and thus β_1 is the range of y, which in this case is $2 - (-2) = 4$. The γ parameters control the location and scale of the logistic function. The center of the logistic function occurs at $-\frac{\gamma_0}{\gamma_1}$, here 0.6. For larger values of γ_1, in the

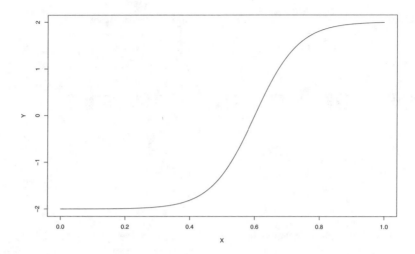

Figure 3.1. *Fitted function with a single hidden node.*

neighborhood of the center, y changes at a steeper rate as x gets farther away from the center. If γ_1 is positive, then the logistic rises from left to right. If γ_1 is negative, then the logistic will decrease as x increases.

Note that a similar interpretation can be used when there are additional explanatory variables, with the γ_0, γ_1, and x above being replaced by a linear combination of the x's with coefficients γ_j, so that the logistic rises with respect to the entire linear combination.

This interpretation scheme can also be extended to additional logistic functions as long as their centers are spaced sufficiently far apart from each other. In that case, for any given value of x, it will be close to the center of at most one logistic, and it will be in the tails of all others (where a small change in x does not produce a noticeable change in y). Thus the parameters of each logistic function can be dealt with separately, using the previous interpretation locally.

Two logistics with opposite signs on γ_1 can be placed so that they are somewhat but not too close to each other, and together they form a bump, jointly acting much like a kernel or a radial basis function. One could attempt to apply some of the interpretations of mixture models here, but in practice, fitted functions rarely behave in this manner.

In most real-world problems, there will be some overlap of the logistic functions, which can lead to many other sorts of behavior in the neural network predictions, effectively removing any interpretability. A simple example is shown in Figure 3.2, which deals with a model with a single explanatory variable and only two hidden nodes (logistic functions).

This example involves fitting the motorcycle accident data of Silverman (1985), which tracks the acceleration force on the head of a motorcycle rider in the first moments after impact. Here a neural network with two hidden nodes was used, and the maximum likelihood fit is shown in Figure 3.2. This model fits the data somewhat well, although it does appear to oversmooth in the first milliseconds after the crash. The point is not that this is the best possible fit but rather that this particular fit, which is the maximum likelihood fit, displays interesting behavior with respect to the parameters of the model. Remember that there are only two logistic functions producing this fit, yet there are three points of inflection in the fitted curve. Thus the previous interpretations of the parameters no longer apply. What is going on here is that the two logistic functions have centers very close to each other, so that their ranges of action interact, and do so in a highly nonlinear fashion. These logistic bases are shown in Figure 3.3. Another manner in which interpretation has disappeared is the scale of the logistics. Notice that the individual logistic functions have a range two orders of magnitude larger than the original data, as well as than the fitted function that they combine to produce. Had one only seen the data and decided to fit a model with two hidden nodes, it is unlikely that one would expect to fit a logistic function with parameters on such a large scale, yet these are the maximum likelihood estimates. From this simple example, it is clear that interpretation can be difficult, and things can get much worse as more logistic functions are added to the model. The reader is thus cautioned to keep this example in mind when considering the choice of prior for a neural network model.

Another example of interpretation difficulties can be found in Robinson (2001a). He provides an example (pp. 19–20) of two fitted three-node neural networks which give very similar fitted curves, yet have completely different parameter values. We again see that there is no clear link between parameter values and their interpretations.

3.2   Proper Priors

Most standard priors for neural networks in the literature are hierarchical proper priors. By *proper*, it means that the prior distribution is a valid probability distribution which puts probability one on the whole domain of the distribution. The alternative is an *improper* distribution, one that does not have a finite measure, as discussed in the next section. A *hierarchical* prior is a multistage prior, with two or more levels of parameters. The higher-level parameters (often called hyperparameters) serve as parameters for the prior distributions of parameters in lower levels. For example, a simple prior for β_0 might be a normal distribution with mean 0 and variance 10. A simple hierarchical version could be a normal distribution with mean 0 and variance τ, where τ has its own prior distribution. The conjugate choice would be an inverse-gamma (recall the discussion of conjugacy in Section 2.4). In both cases, the prior mean $E[\beta_0] = 0$, but the prior variance for β_0 will be different, as will the shape of the distribution. The hierarchical version dilutes the information put in at the top level so that the resulting prior for β_0 is more diffuse (in the conjugate case, the marginal prior when σ is integrated out is a t distribution). For more details on hierarchical priors, the reader is referred to a Bayesian text, such as Gelman et al. (1995). Hierarchical priors are useful for neural networks because of the lack of interpretability of the parameters. As the addition of levels to the prior reduces the influence of the particular choice made at the top level, the resulting prior at the bottom level (the

Fit with 2 Hidden Nodes

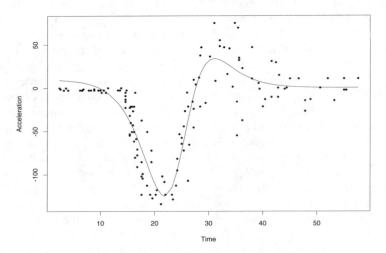

Figure 3.2. *Maximum likelihood fit for a two-hidden node network.*

Individual Nodes

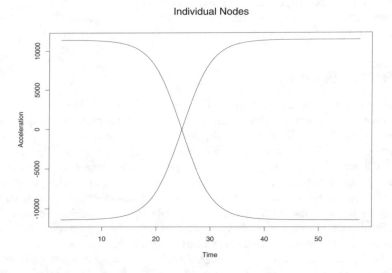

Figure 3.3. *Logistic basis functions of the fit in Figure* 3.2.

original parameters) will be more diffuse, more closely matching the lack of information we really have about the parameters themselves. This approach lets the data have more influence on the posterior. Let us now take a look at several proposed hierarchical priors.

Müller and Rios Insua (1998) proposed a three-stage hierarchical model with a relatively simple structure, although many parameters are multivariate. Prior distributions are

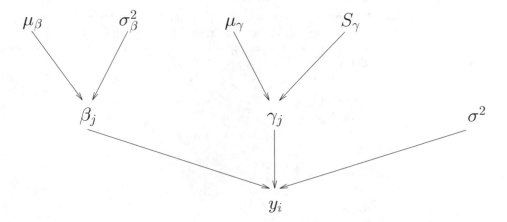

Figure 3.4. *DAG for the Müller and Rios Insua model.*

chosen to be conditionally conjugate, which will help in fitting the model (see Section 3.5). The distributions for parameters and hyperparameters are

$$y_i \sim N\left(\sum_{j=0}^{k} \beta_j \Psi(\boldsymbol{\gamma}_j' \mathbf{x}_i), \sigma^2\right), \quad i = 1, \ldots, N,$$

$$\beta_j \sim N(\mu_\beta, \sigma_\beta^2), \quad j = 0, \ldots, k,$$

$$\boldsymbol{\gamma}_j \sim N_p(\mu_\gamma, \mathbf{S}_\gamma), \quad j = 1, \ldots, k,$$

$$\mu_\beta \sim N(a_\beta, A_\beta),$$

$$\mu_\gamma \sim N_p(a_\gamma, \mathbf{A}_\gamma),$$

$$\sigma_\beta^2 \sim \Gamma^{-1}\left(\frac{c_\beta}{2}, \frac{C_\beta}{2}\right),$$

$$\mathbf{S}_\gamma \sim Wish^{-1}(c_\gamma, (c_\gamma \mathbf{C}_\gamma)^{-1}),$$

$$\sigma^2 \sim \Gamma^{-1}\left(\frac{s}{2}, \frac{S}{2}\right),$$

where a_β, A_β, a_γ, $\mathbf{A}_\gamma$, c_β, C_β, c_γ, $\mathbf{C}_\gamma$, s, and S are constants that need to be chosen a priori.

A tool for visualizing a hierarchical prior is a directed acyclic graph (DAG), where the arrows show the flow of dependency. Figure 3.4 shows the DAG for this model. The parameters of the network (β, γ, and σ) are near the bottom of the graph, with their hyperparameters above. The hyperparameters have prior distributions with constants that need to be specified. Müller and Rios Insua suggest setting many of them to be of the same scale as the data. As some fitting algorithms work better when (or sometimes only when) the data have been rescaled so that $|x_{ih}|, |y_i| \leq 1$ (Ripley (1996)), for rescaled data one choice of starting hyperparameters is $a_\beta = 0$, $A_\beta = 1$, $a_\gamma = \mathbf{0}$, $\mathbf{A}_\gamma = \mathbf{I}_p$, $c_\beta = 1$, $C_\beta = 1$, $c_\gamma = p + 1$, $\mathbf{C}_\gamma = \frac{1}{p+1}\mathbf{I}_p$, $s = 1$, $S = \frac{1}{10}$.

Neal (1996) suggests a more complex model, although all parameters are univariate. He also uses hyperbolic tangent activation functions rather than logistic functions. These are essentially equivalent in terms of the neural network, as discussed in Section 2.3.5. A simple version of the model is

$$
y_i \sim N\left(\beta_0 + \sum_{j=1}^{k} \beta_j \tanh(\boldsymbol{\gamma}_j' \mathbf{x}_i), \sigma^2\right), \qquad i = 1, \ldots, N,
$$

$$
\begin{aligned}
\beta_0 &\sim N(0, \sigma_{b,o}\sigma_{a,o}), \\
\beta_j &\sim N(0, \sigma_{out,j}\sigma_{a,o}), & j &= 1, \ldots, k, \\
\gamma_{j,0} &\sim N(0, \sigma_{b,in}\sigma_{a,j}), & j &= 1, \ldots, k, \\
\gamma_{j,h} &\sim N(0, \sigma_{in,h}\sigma_{a,j}), & j &= 1, \ldots, k, \quad h = 1, \ldots, r, \\
\sigma_{b,o}^2 &\sim \Gamma^{-1}\left(\frac{\alpha_b}{2}, \frac{\alpha_b}{2\omega_b}\right), \\
\sigma_{b,in}^2 &\sim \Gamma^{-1}\left(\frac{\alpha_b}{2}, \frac{\alpha_b}{2\omega_b}\right), \\
\sigma_{a,o}^2 &\sim \Gamma^{-1}\left(\frac{\alpha_a}{2}, \frac{\alpha_a}{2\omega_a}\right), \\
\sigma_{a,j}^2 &\sim \Gamma^{-1}\left(\frac{\alpha_a}{2}, \frac{\alpha_a}{2\omega_a}\right), & j &= 1, \ldots, k, \\
\sigma_{in,h}^2 &\sim \Gamma^{-1}\left(\frac{\alpha_1}{2}, \frac{\alpha_1 \sigma_{in}^2}{2}\right), & h &= 1, \ldots, r, \\
\sigma_{out,j}^2 &\sim \Gamma^{-1}\left(\frac{\alpha_1}{2}, \frac{\alpha_1 \sigma_{out}^2}{2}\right), & j &= 1, \ldots, k, \\
\sigma_{in}^2 &\sim \Gamma^{-1}\left(\frac{\alpha_0}{2}, \frac{\alpha_0}{2\omega_0}\right), \\
\sigma_{out}^2 &\sim \Gamma^{-1}\left(\frac{\alpha_0}{2}, \frac{\alpha_0}{2\omega_0}\right), \\
\sigma^2 &\sim \Gamma^{-1}\left(\frac{\alpha_2}{2}, \frac{\alpha_2}{2\omega_y}\right),
\end{aligned}
$$

where α_0, α_1, α_2, α_a, α_b, ω_0, ω_a, and ω_b are constants to be specified. As it appears in Neal (1996), this model contains additional generalizations such as multiple hidden layers and connections from all hidden layers to the output. A DAG diagram of the model is shown in Figure 3.5. Each of the original network parameters (β and γ) is treated as a univariate normal with mean zero and its own variance. These variances are the product of two hyperparameters, one for the originating node of the link in the graph and one for the destination node. For example, the weight for the first input to the first hidden node, γ_{11}, has distribution $N\left(0, \sigma_{in,1} * \sigma_{a,1}\right)$, where $\sigma_{in,h}$ is the term for the links from the hth input, and $\sigma_{a,j}$ is the term for the links into the jth hidden node; the weight from the first hidden node to the output (i.e., the regression coefficient), β_1, has distribution $N\left(0, \sigma_{out,1} * \sigma_o\right)$, where $\sigma_{out,j}$ is the term for the links from the jth hidden node, and σ_o is the term for links to the output node. For all of the new σ parameters and for the original σ of the error term, there is an inverse-gamma distribution. There is another set of hyperparameters that must be specified for the inverse-gamma priors on these σ parameters.

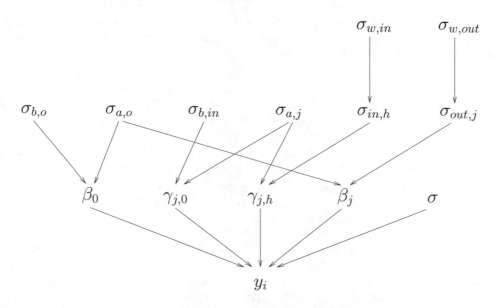

Figure 3.5. *DAG for the Neal model.*

The version of the model presented here is for a univariate response; this model extends to multivariate responses and classification by adding an additional output unit for each dimension of the response and extending the hierarchy to account for additional output units. One further note on this model is that Neal also discusses using t distributions instead of normal distributions for the parameters, resulting in a more robust model.

3.3   Noninformative Priors

As was demonstrated in Section 3.1, the parameters of a neural network are typically not interpretable. This makes choosing an informative prior difficult. The previous section introduced various hierarchical priors. These priors were defined to be proper, yet an attempt was made to let them be diffuse enough that they did not contain too much information, since one would not want to use a highly informative prior that may not come close to one's actual beliefs, or lack thereof. An alternative approach is to use a noninformative prior, one that attempts to quantify ignorance about the parameters in some manner.

There are a variety of ways to attempt to represent ignorance. Early work on non-informative priors was done by Jeffreys (1961). Kass and Wasserman (1996) provide a thorough review of this extensive literature. Many noninformative priors, including those in this chapter, have invariance properties (Hartigan (1964)). For example, the Jeffreys prior (Jeffreys (1961)) is invariant with respect to all differentiable transformations of the input variables.

In many cases, such as for a neural network, procedures for creating a noninformative prior result in a prior that is improper, in the sense that the integral of its density is infinite.

While this may sound alarming, it is not a problem as long as the posterior is proper. A simple example of an improper noninformative prior with a proper posterior is the following: We have n observations y_i which are normally distributed with unknown mean μ and variance 1, i.e., $y_1, \ldots, y_n \overset{iid}{\sim} N(\mu, 1)$. We want to use a prior for μ that does not favor any values a priori (i.e., it does not have any information in it), and the common approach is to say that the prior is flat over the whole real line, e.g., $P(\mu) = 1$, which is equivalent to using Lebesgue measure (this prior can also be thought of as a limiting case of a normal distribution with infinite variance). Note that as long as the density function is constant, it does not matter to what finite value it is set. Clearly $\int_{\Re} P(\mu)\, d\mu = \infty$, so the prior is improper. However, formal application of Bayes' theorem, $p(\mu|\mathbf{y}) = \frac{P(\mu, \mathbf{y})}{P(\mathbf{y})}$, shows that the posterior for μ is normal with mean $\bar{y}$ and variance $\frac{1}{n}$, so the posterior is proper and the posterior mean is the maximum likelihood estimate. For this simple problem, a flat prior is an easy way to represent ignorance, and the resulting posterior depends only on the data, the ideal situation when one has no prior beliefs.

As a second example, consider the case of (multiple) linear regression, $y_i = \beta_0 + \beta_1 x_{1i} + \cdots + \beta_k x_{ki} + \varepsilon_i, \varepsilon_i \sim N(0, \sigma^2)$. The parameters here are the coefficients, $\beta_0, \ldots, \beta_k$, and the variance, σ^2. For the slope coefficients, the standard noninformative prior is a flat prior, just as in the simple normal example above. For the variance, as variances must be positive and one might expect them to be skewed, the standard choice is to use a flat prior on the log of the variance, which is equivalent to using $P(\sigma^2) \propto \frac{1}{\sigma^2}$, and has the added bonus of being conjugate. Note that it can be simpler to think of the variance as the parameter (or the precision, which is the reciprocal of the variance), rather than the standard deviation. The resulting posterior is always proper, as long as there are a sufficient number of linearly independent data points (just as would be required to fit a classical least-squares regression). A noninformative prior such as this one leaves all fitting of location and scale to the data. The posterior mean for the coefficients is again the same as the maximum likelihood solutions, which is often, but not always, the case for flat priors. Gelman et al. (1995) present some theoretical advantages of this family of priors.

Unfortunately, for neural networks, standard noninformative priors lead to improper posteriors, so we will need to take care as we move on to look at some possible representations of ignorance. The next sections will present three possible approaches, in increasing levels of complication.

3.3.1   Flat Priors

Just as in the simple normal example and the regression example above, a flat prior can be applied to the parameters of a neural network. As the β parameters of a neural network are analogous to regression coefficients (for fixed values of the γ's, fitting the β's is exactly a linear regression problem), it is reasonable to consider a flat prior for them. A flat prior on the log of the variance is also natural by the same reasoning. The prior for the γ parameters is a more tender question, as they are the ones that are particularly lacking in interpretation. One obvious approach is to also use a flat prior for them. The resulting flat prior for all parameters is

$$P(\boldsymbol{\gamma}, \boldsymbol{\beta}, \sigma^2) \propto \frac{1}{\sigma^2}. \tag{3.1}$$

Since the prior is improper, it does not change when multiplied by a constant, so the constant 1 is used here to keep things simple.

There is a major problem with this prior. It leads to an improper posterior, and so in this form it is not useful. It turns out that there are two ways in which things can go wrong: linear independence and tail behavior. It will be shown (equation (3.2)) that by restricting this prior, one can guarantee that the posterior will be proper. The discussion of this prior first appeared in Lee (2003).

Some notation will be helpful. Denote the basis functions evaluated at the data points (i.e., the outputs of the hidden layer) as

$$z_{ij} = \left[1 + \exp\left(-\gamma_{j0} - \sum_{h=1}^{r} \gamma_{jh} x_{ih} \right) \right]^{-1}$$

with $z_{i0} = 1$, and let $\mathbf{Z}$ be the matrix with elements (z_{ij}). Thus the fitting of the vector $\boldsymbol{\beta}$ is a least-squares regression on the design matrix $\mathbf{Z}$.

To understand the linear independence problem, we continue the linear regression parallel. When using the standard noninformative prior for linear regression, the posterior will be proper as long as the design matrix is full rank (its columns are linearly independent); i.e., for a regression problem with p parameters, the posterior will be proper as long as there are at least p observations that do not all lie on the same $(p-1)$-dimensional hyperplane. Thus, for a neural network, we need the k logistic basis functions to be linearly independent; i.e., we need $\mathbf{Z}$ to be full rank. A straightforward way to ensure linear independence is to require that the determinant of $\mathbf{Z}'\mathbf{Z}$ is positive, as will be explained below.

The second possible posterior propriety problem is that the likelihood does not necessarily go to zero in the tails, converging to various nonzero constants. If the tails of the prior also do not go to zero as the parameter values go off to infinity, the tails of the posterior will similarly fail to go to zero, and thus the posterior will not have a finite integral unless the parameter space is bounded. An obvious way to avoid this problem is to bound the parameter space. Details will be discussed below and in Section 3.7.

How do these problems manifest themselves in a neural network model? We first consider a simplified problem with indicator functions to illustrate how things can go wrong, and then we return to the case of neural networks. Suppose we are looking at a simplified neural network that uses indicator (also called threshold or Heaviside) functions instead of logistic functions, i.e.,

$$\Psi_j(x) = I_{\{x \le a_j\}} \quad \text{or} \quad \Psi_j(x) = I_{\{x > a_j\}},$$

where $I_{\{\}}$ is an indicator function, equal to one when its argument is true, zero otherwise. As a further simplification, suppose that the network contains only two hidden nodes. When we condition on the hidden nodes, we are then fitting a linear regression on the terms $\mathbf{z}_j = (z_{1j}, \ldots, z_{nj}) = (1, \ldots, 1, 0, \ldots, 0)$ or $(0, \ldots, 0, 1, \ldots, 1)$ and $\mathbf{z}_0 = (1, \ldots, 1)$ (providing the constant term, also called a bias input). Let

$$v_i = \sum_j z_{ij} \quad \text{for } i = 1, 2; \qquad v_{12} = \sum_j z_{1j} z_{2j}.$$

The quantity v_1 is the number of cases whose first explanatory variable is larger (or smaller depending on the direction of inequality in the indicator) than the first threshold a_1, and v_{12}

is the number of cases for which both explanatory variables are beyond their thresholds. Recall that to ensure linear independence we can require that the determinant of $\mathbf{Z}^t\mathbf{Z}$ be positive. Note that

$$|\mathbf{Z}^t\mathbf{Z}| = \begin{vmatrix} v_1 & v_{12} & v_1 \\ v_{12} & v_2 & v_2 \\ v_1 & v_2 & n \end{vmatrix} = v_1 v_2 n + 2 v_1 v_2 v_{12} - v_1^2 v_2 - v_1 v_2^2 - v_{12}^2 n.$$

This determinant will be zero if any of the following happen: $v_i = 0$, $v_i = n$, $v_1 = v_2 = v_{12}$, or $\{v_1 = n - v_2 \text{ and } v_{12} = 0\}$. The key idea is that the thresholds for the indicator functions must all be separated by data points (i.e., there is a data point x_i that is between the thresholds of the two indicators) and that no threshold occurs outside the range of the data. These are exactly the conditions that prevent linear dependence in the z_j's. Thus, by requiring that $|\mathbf{Z}^t\mathbf{Z}| > 0$, we can guarantee linear independence. The same logic applies to datasets with more inputs and to networks with more hidden nodes. These sorts of restrictions are now common in the mixture model literature (Diebolt and Robert (1994); Wasserman (2000)).

For indicator function basis functions, the requirement on the determinant also prevents impropriety in the posterior. Consider the case of trying to fit an indicator function where the parameter is the threshold. Suppose one tries to fit a threshold smaller than the smallest data point, x_{min}. Then the data do not provide any information for distinguishing between putting the threshold at $x_{min} - b_1$ and $x_{min} - b_2$ for any positive numbers b_1 and b_2. Thus the set of thresholds strictly less than x_{min} is an uncountably large equivalence set which leads to an issue of identifiability. Since this set has infinite mass under a flat prior, the posterior is improper. On the other hand, when fitting a threshold inside the range of the data, the data force propriety on the posterior. Thus the linear independence condition, and hence the determinant condition, resolve this possible source of impropriety.

How does this relate to a neural network with logistic basis functions? Indicator functions are a limiting case of logistic functions. Let

$$\Psi(x) = \frac{1}{1 + \exp(-\gamma_0 - \gamma_1 x)}$$

be a logistic function. If $\gamma_0, \gamma_1 \to \infty$ such that $\frac{\gamma_0}{\gamma_1} \to a$ for some constant a, then $\Psi(x) \to I_{\{x > -a\}}$ (for $\gamma_1 > 0$). Thus the logistic can turn into an indicator for large values of the parameters. We then require the determinant condition to guarantee linear independence.

However, recall that there are two possible problems with propriety. The second occurs in the triangular region where $\gamma_0, \gamma_1 \to \infty$ such that $\frac{\gamma_0}{\gamma_1} \to a$, which has infinite area. Over this region, as the parameters get large, the likelihood converges to some nonzero constant (in most problems, the likelihood converges to zero in the tails). With a flat prior, the posterior over this region alone is improper. Analogous problems can happen in higher dimensions, as will be detailed in Section 3.3.2. For this reason, we also need to bound the individual γ_{jh} parameters, $|\gamma_{jh}| < D$. It can also be helpful to bound the β_j parameters for reasons of numerical stability during computations. Bounds will also be necessary for asymptotic consistency as described in Section 3.7.

The logistic functions allow values between zero and one so that two columns of $\mathbf{Z}^t\mathbf{Z}$ could be very similar but not identical. This condition is known as multicollinearity in the context of regression. The near-linear dependence causes instability in the parameter estimates. It is computationally desirable to avoid this case, which we can do by requiring the determinant to be larger than some small positive number C rather than merely requiring it to be nonzero. Again, asymptotic consistency will also require a bound $C > 0$, as described in Section 3.7. We may wish to set the value of C based on the sample size n, and we refer to this bound as C_n. For example, we might pick $C_n = \frac{1}{n}$.

From a practical standpoint, it is worth noting that truncating the parameter space need not have much impact on the posterior, as the fitted functions being eliminated are not numerically distinguishable from those in the valid range of the parameter space. For example, consider a single logistic function, $\Psi(z) = 1/(1 + \exp(z))$. If the argument z is larger than 40 or so, the logistic will return 1.0 in double precision. Similarly, if it is less than -750, it will return 0 in double precision. Thus large γ parameter values become redundant after a certain point, and nothing is lost in truncating their space, as long as the truncation point is sufficiently large (which will depend on the scale of the data).

Thus instead of using the flat prior of equation (3.1), a restricted prior should be used:

$$P_n(\boldsymbol{\gamma}, \boldsymbol{\beta}, \sigma^2) = P(\boldsymbol{\gamma}, \boldsymbol{\beta}, \sigma^2) I_{\{(\boldsymbol{\gamma}, \boldsymbol{\beta}, \sigma^2) \in \boldsymbol{\Omega}_n\}} \propto \frac{1}{\sigma^2} I_{\{(\boldsymbol{\gamma}, \boldsymbol{\beta}, \sigma^2) \in \boldsymbol{\Omega}_n\}}, \qquad (3.2)$$

where $I_{\{\}}$ is an indicator function, and $\boldsymbol{\Omega}_n$ is the parameter space restricted such that

1. $|\mathbf{Z}^T \mathbf{Z}| > C_n$,

2. $|\gamma_{jh}| < D_n$ for all j, h,

3. $|\beta_j| < D_n$ for all j,

where $C_n > 0$ and $D_n > 0$ are constants which can depend on the sample size n (with C_n small and D_n large).

Now we prove that the restricted prior, P_n of equation (3.2), leads to a proper posterior. Denote the likelihood by L_n (e.g., equation (2.6)), and denote the vector of all parameters by $\boldsymbol{\theta} = (\boldsymbol{\gamma}, \boldsymbol{\beta}, \sigma^2)$. Let P be the unrestricted noninformative prior of equation (3.1), P_n be the restricted prior, and $\boldsymbol{\Omega}_n$ be the restricted parameter space described after equation (3.2). Let C_n decrease to 0 as n gets large (for example, $C_n = 1/n$), and let D_n increase with n (for example, $D_n = 100,000 + n$). First, we factor the likelihood so that we can integrate out $\boldsymbol{\beta}$, which involves completing the square for $\boldsymbol{\beta}$:

$$L_n = f(\boldsymbol{\beta}, \boldsymbol{\gamma}, \sigma | \mathbf{y}) = (2\pi\sigma^2)^{-n/2} \exp\left[-\frac{1}{2\sigma^2} \sum_{i=1}^{n} \left(\sum_{j=0}^{k} \beta_j z_j - y_i \right)^2 \right]$$

in vector notation:

$$= (2\pi\sigma^2)^{-n/2} \exp\left[-\frac{1}{2\sigma^2} (\mathbf{Z}\boldsymbol{\beta} - \mathbf{Y})^t (\mathbf{Z}\boldsymbol{\beta} - \mathbf{Y}) \right]$$

$$= (2\pi\sigma^2)^{-\frac{k+1}{2}} |\mathbf{Z}^t\mathbf{Z}|^{-\frac{1}{2}} \exp\left\{ -\frac{1}{2\sigma^2} \left[\boldsymbol{\beta} - (\mathbf{Z}^t\mathbf{Z})^{-1}\mathbf{Z}^t\mathbf{Y} \right]^t (\mathbf{Z}^t\mathbf{Z}) \left[\boldsymbol{\beta} - (\mathbf{Z}^t\mathbf{Z})^{-1}\mathbf{Z}^t\mathbf{Y} \right] \right\} *$$

$$(2\pi\sigma^2)^{-\frac{n-(k+1)}{2}} |\mathbf{Z}^t\mathbf{Z}|^{\frac{1}{2}} \exp\left\{ -\frac{1}{2\sigma^2} \left[\mathbf{Y}^t\mathbf{Y} - \hat{\mathbf{Y}}^t\hat{\mathbf{Y}} \right] \right\}$$

$$= f(\boldsymbol{\beta} | \boldsymbol{\gamma}, \sigma, \mathbf{y}) f(\boldsymbol{\gamma}, \sigma | \mathbf{y}),$$

where $\hat{\mathbf{Y}}$ is the vector of fitted values, $\hat{\mathbf{Y}} = E[\mathbf{Y}|\mathbf{X}]$. Note that $f(\boldsymbol{\beta}|\boldsymbol{\gamma}, \sigma, \mathbf{y})$ is a proper density as long as $|\mathbf{Z}^t\mathbf{Z}| > 0$, which is true over Ω_n. Denote by Γ_n the subspace of Ω_n that relates to all of the $\boldsymbol{\gamma}$ parameters. We next integrate out $\boldsymbol{\beta}$ and σ^2:

$$
\begin{aligned}
\int L_n P_n &= \int_{\Omega_n} f(\boldsymbol{\beta}|\boldsymbol{\gamma}, \sigma, \mathbf{y}) f(\boldsymbol{\gamma}, \sigma|\mathbf{y}) \left[\frac{1}{\sigma^2}\right] d\boldsymbol{\beta} d\sigma d\boldsymbol{\gamma} \\
&= \int_{\Gamma_n} \int \left[\int f(\boldsymbol{\beta}|\boldsymbol{\gamma}, \sigma, \mathbf{y}) d\boldsymbol{\beta}\right] \frac{1}{\sigma^2} f(\boldsymbol{\gamma}, \sigma|\mathbf{y}) d\sigma d\boldsymbol{\gamma} \\
&= \int_{\Gamma_n} \int \frac{1}{\sigma^2} (2\pi\sigma^2)^{-\frac{n-(k+1)}{2}} |\mathbf{Z}^t\mathbf{Z}|^{\frac{1}{2}} \exp\left\{-\frac{1}{2\sigma^2}\left[\mathbf{Y}^t\mathbf{Y} - \hat{\mathbf{Y}}^t\hat{\mathbf{Y}}\right]\right\} d\sigma d\boldsymbol{\gamma} \\
&\leq \int_{\Gamma_n} \int \frac{1}{\sigma^2} (2\pi\sigma^2)^{-\frac{n-(k+1)}{2}} |\mathbf{Z}^t\mathbf{Z}|^{\frac{1}{2}} d\sigma d\boldsymbol{\gamma} \\
&= (2\pi)^{-\frac{n-(k+1)}{2}} (n-k+1)^{-1} \int_{\Gamma_n} |\mathbf{Z}^t\mathbf{Z}|^{\frac{1}{2}} d\boldsymbol{\gamma}.
\end{aligned}
$$

The last integral is finite because Γ_n is a bounded set and the integrand is finite. Thus the posterior is guaranteed to be proper.

The most important thing is to know that the posterior will be proper. But if using a modified prior produces a posterior that is very different from what one would have gotten from the original prior, that would also be bad. In practice, the "interesting" parts of the parameter space are the same under the restricted and unrestricted priors, and thus the posteriors are the same. We can also show two asymptotic equivalence properties, a global one and a local one, meaning that the restricted prior is asymptotically equivalent to the original improper prior.

For a global perspective, first consider integrating the absolute difference of the priors over an arbitrary compact set κ:

$$
\int_\kappa |P_n - P| = \int_\kappa \left|P I_{\Omega_n} - P\right| \to 0 \text{ as } n \to \infty
$$

because $|\mathbf{Z}^t\mathbf{Z}|$ must be nonzero for the true function (or else it would have one fewer node), and, because for a large enough n, Ω_n will contain all elements of κ that satisfy the determinant condition. This equation says that, in the limit as the sample size grows, P_n converges to P on all compact sets. In this sense, the two priors are "asymptotically globally equivalent" (Wasserman (2000)).

The second condition is "asymptotic local equivalence," which relates to second-order frequentist coverage properties (Wasserman (2000)). The idea is that the original and restricted priors have the same local properties (while the restricted prior is better behaved in the tails). Suppose there exists a true value of the parameters, $\boldsymbol{\theta}_0$. Then, for large n,

$$
\left|\frac{\partial \log P_n}{\partial \boldsymbol{\theta}_0} - \frac{\partial \log P}{\partial \boldsymbol{\theta}_0}\right| = O_p\left(\frac{1}{\sqrt{n}}\right)
$$

because if n is large enough, $\boldsymbol{\theta}_0$ will be contained in Ω_n.

3.3.2 Jeffreys Priors

Flat priors are not without drawbacks. In particular, if the problem is reparameterized using a nonlinear one-to-one transformation of the parameters, then the same transformation applied to the prior will result in something other than a flat prior. Jeffreys (1946; 1961) introduced a rule for generating a prior that is invariant to differentiable one-to-one transformations of the parameters. The Jeffreys prior is the square root of the determinant of the Fisher information matrix:

$$P_J(\boldsymbol{\theta}) = \sqrt{|I(\boldsymbol{\theta})|}, \tag{3.3}$$

where under certain regularity conditions the Fisher information matrix, $I(\boldsymbol{\theta})$, has elements

$$I_{ij}(\boldsymbol{\theta}) = -E_{\boldsymbol{\theta}} \left[\frac{\partial^2}{\partial \theta_i \partial \theta_j} \log f(\mathbf{Y}|\boldsymbol{\theta}) \right],$$

where $f(\mathbf{Y}|\boldsymbol{\theta})$ is the likelihood and the expectation is over $\mathbf{Y}$ for fixed $\boldsymbol{\theta}$. In many problems, the Jeffreys prior is intuitively reasonable and leads to a proper posterior. However, there are some known situations where the prior seems unreasonable or fails to produce a reasonable or even proper posterior (see, for example, Jeffreys (1961), Berger and Bernardo (1992), Berger, De Oliveira, and Sansó (2001), or Schervish (1995, pp. 122–123)). We will see that we have problems with posterior impropriety with the Jeffreys prior for a neural network.

Jeffreys (1961) made arguments that it is often better to treat classes of parameters as independent and compute the priors independently (treating parameters from other classes as fixed during the computation). To distinguish this approach from the previous one which treated all parameters collectively, the collective prior (equation (3.3)) is referred to as the *Jeffreys-rule prior*. In contrast, the *independence Jeffreys prior* (denoted P_{IJ}) is the product of the Jeffreys-rule priors for each class of parameters independently, while treating the other parameters as fixed. In the case of a neural network, separate Jeffreys-rule priors would be computed for each of $\boldsymbol{\gamma}$, $\boldsymbol{\beta}$, and σ^2, and the independence Jeffreys prior is the product of these separate priors.

In some problems, such as linear regression and neural network models, the Jeffreys prior will depend on part of the data, the explanatory variables. This is because the Fisher information depends on the explanatory variables (e.g., in linear regression, the data hold more information when the points are farther apart). Note that in a regression situation, we typically consider the explanatory variables as fixed, and it is only the response part of the data that is considered random.

The next step is to compute the Fisher information matrix. We shall consider only univariate regression predictions here, but these results can be extended to a multivariate regression or classification scenario. Recall that the predicted value for a neural network regression is

$$\hat{y}_i = \beta_0 + \sum_{j=1}^{k} \beta_j \Psi(\boldsymbol{\gamma}_j^t \mathbf{x}_i),$$

and so the vector of predictions for all cases can be written in matrix form as

$$\hat{\mathbf{y}} = \boldsymbol{\Gamma}^t \boldsymbol{\beta},$$

where $\boldsymbol{\Gamma}$ is an n x $(k+1)$ matrix with elements $\Gamma_{i0} = 1$ and

$$\Gamma_{ij} = \frac{1}{1 + \exp\left(-\gamma_{j0} - \sum_{h=1}^{r} \gamma_{jh}x_{ih}\right)} \tag{3.4}$$

for $j = 1, \ldots, k$, and can be seen as a transformation of the explanatory variables and the $\boldsymbol{\gamma}$ parameters. Written in this form, it is also obvious that conditioned on $\boldsymbol{\gamma}$, fitting $\boldsymbol{\beta}$ is exactly a linear regression problem. For notational and conceptual simplicity, it is easier to work with the precision, $\tau = \frac{1}{\sigma^2}$, the reciprocal of the variance, than it is to work directly with the variance. Thus our parameter vector is $\boldsymbol{\theta} = (\boldsymbol{\gamma}, \boldsymbol{\beta}, \tau)$, and the full likelihood is

$$f(\mathbf{y}|\boldsymbol{\theta}) = f(\mathbf{y}|\mathbf{x}, \boldsymbol{\gamma}, \boldsymbol{\beta}, \tau) = (2\pi)^{-n/2}\tau^{n/2} \exp\left\{-\frac{\tau}{2}(\mathbf{y} - \boldsymbol{\Gamma}'\boldsymbol{\beta})'(\mathbf{y} - \boldsymbol{\Gamma}'\boldsymbol{\beta})\right\} .$$

The loglikelihood, without the normalizing constant, is

$$\log f = \frac{n}{2} \log \tau - \frac{\tau}{2}(\mathbf{y} - \boldsymbol{\Gamma}'\boldsymbol{\beta})'(\mathbf{y} - \boldsymbol{\Gamma}'\boldsymbol{\beta}) .$$

Formally, the Fisher information matrix, $I(\boldsymbol{\theta})$, has elements

$$I_{ij}(\boldsymbol{\theta}) = \text{Cov}_{\boldsymbol{\theta}}\left[\left(\frac{\partial}{\partial\theta_i} \log f(\mathbf{y}|\boldsymbol{\theta})\right)\left(\frac{\partial}{\partial\theta_j} \log f(\mathbf{y}|\boldsymbol{\theta})\right)\right] .$$

Under certain regularity conditions (see, for example, Schervish (1995, p. 111)), which do hold for neural networks, the elements can also be written

$$I_{ij}(\boldsymbol{\theta}) = -E_{\boldsymbol{\theta}}\left[\frac{\partial^2}{\partial\theta_i\partial\theta_j} \log f(\mathbf{y}|\boldsymbol{\theta})\right] .$$

We now compute each of the elements of the information matrix for a neural network model. Using the Γ_{ij} notation from equation (3.4), it is straightforward (if tedious) to show that

$$Cov_{\boldsymbol{\theta}}\left(\frac{\partial}{\partial\beta_j} \log f(\mathbf{y}|\boldsymbol{\theta}), \frac{\partial}{\partial\beta_g} \log f(\mathbf{y}|\boldsymbol{\theta})\right) = \tau \sum_{i=1}^{n} \Gamma_{ij}\Gamma_{ig},$$

$$Cov_{\boldsymbol{\theta}}\left(\frac{\partial}{\partial\beta_j} \log f(\mathbf{y}|\boldsymbol{\theta}), \frac{\partial}{\partial\gamma_{gh}} \log f(\mathbf{y}|\boldsymbol{\theta})\right) = \tau\beta_g \sum_{i=1}^{n} x_{ih}\Gamma_{ij}\Gamma_{ig}(1 - \Gamma_{ig}),$$

$$Cov_{\boldsymbol{\theta}}\left(\frac{\partial}{\partial\gamma_{jh}} \log f(\mathbf{y}|\boldsymbol{\theta}), \frac{\partial}{\partial\gamma_{gl}} \log f(\mathbf{y}|\boldsymbol{\theta})\right) = \tau\beta_j\beta_g \sum_{i=1}^{n} x_{ih}x_{il}\Gamma_{ij}(1 - \Gamma_{ij})\Gamma_{ig}(1 - \Gamma_{ig}),$$

$$Cov_{\boldsymbol{\theta}}\left(\frac{\partial}{\partial\beta_j} \log f(\mathbf{y}|\boldsymbol{\theta}), \frac{\partial}{\partial\tau} \log f(\mathbf{y}|\boldsymbol{\theta})\right) = 0,$$

$$Cov_{\boldsymbol{\theta}}\left(\frac{\partial}{\partial\gamma_{jh}} \log f(\mathbf{y}|\boldsymbol{\theta}), \frac{\partial}{\partial\tau} \log f(\mathbf{y}|\boldsymbol{\theta})\right) = 0,$$

$$Var_{\boldsymbol{\theta}}\left(\frac{\partial}{\partial\tau} \log f(\mathbf{y}|\boldsymbol{\theta})\right) = \frac{n}{2\tau^2} .$$

To combine these into the matrix $I(\theta)$, we need to specify the exact ordering of parameters within $\theta = (\gamma, \beta, \tau)$. Obviously, the β section of $k+1$ elements are $(\beta_0, \ldots, \beta_k)$ and the final element is τ, but γ is a matrix, and it could be turned into a vector either in row-order or column-order. In the presentation here, it appears as row-order so that $\gamma = (\gamma_{10}, \gamma_{11}, \gamma_{12}, \ldots, \gamma_{1r}, \gamma_{20}, \gamma_{21}, \ldots, \gamma_{2r}, \gamma_{30}, \gamma_{31}, \ldots)$. Now define the n x $(r+1)k$ matrix $\mathbf{G}$ to have elements

$$G_{ij} = \beta_g x_{ih} \Gamma_{ig}(1 - \Gamma_{ig}), \tag{3.5}$$

where g is the integer part of $\frac{j}{r+1}$ and h is the remainder, i.e., $h = j - (r+1) * g$. Once you understand the notation, it is easy to see that the full Fisher information matrix is

$$I(\theta) = \begin{bmatrix} \tau \mathbf{G}'\mathbf{G} & \tau \mathbf{G}'\boldsymbol{\Gamma} & 0 \\ \tau \boldsymbol{\Gamma}'\mathbf{G} & \tau \boldsymbol{\Gamma}'\boldsymbol{\Gamma} & 0 \\ 0 & 0 & \frac{n}{2\tau^2} \end{bmatrix}. \tag{3.6}$$

Thus the Jeffreys-rule prior is

$$P_J(\theta) \propto \tau^{((r+2)k-1)/2} \left| \begin{matrix} \mathbf{G}'\mathbf{G} & \mathbf{G}'\boldsymbol{\Gamma} \\ \boldsymbol{\Gamma}'\mathbf{G} & \boldsymbol{\Gamma}'\boldsymbol{\Gamma} \end{matrix} \right|^{1/2}. \tag{3.7}$$

The prior is stated as a proportionality because any constants are irrelevant since the prior is improper. The large power on τ seems rather odd, and so Jeffreys would probably recommend the independence prior instead, as this situation is similar to the linear regression setting where analogous problems occur with the prior for the precision. The independence Jeffreys prior is simpler in form, as the Jeffreys-rule prior for β with other parameters fixed is a flat prior:

$$P_{IJ}(\theta) \propto \frac{1}{\tau} |\mathbf{F}'\mathbf{F}|^{1/2}, \tag{3.8}$$

where $\mathbf{F}$ is just $\mathbf{G}$ without any of the β_g terms, i.e., $F_{ij} = x_{ih}\Gamma_{ig}(1 - \Gamma_{ig})$, where g is the integer part of $\frac{j}{r+1}$ and h is the remainder. It is unfortunate that both of these priors are improper, and both lead to improper posteriors. Here is an example of how things can go wrong. Let $\tilde{x}$ be the median of $\{x_{11}, \ldots, x_{n1}\}$, and let $x^* = \max\{x_{12}, \ldots, x_{n2}, x_{13}, \ldots, x_{nr}\}$. For simplicity, assume that $\tilde{x} > 0$ (there is a symmetric argument if it is negative, and the argument can be modified if it is zero). Let $\gamma_{10} \to \infty$ and $\gamma_{11} \to -\infty$ such that $|\gamma_{10} + \gamma_{11}\tilde{x}| < 10^{-r}$, let $|\gamma_{j1} - 2^j| < 10^{-r}$ for $j > 1$, and let all the other γ_{jh} be such that $0 < \gamma_{jh} < (10^r x^*)^{-1}$. Now note that

$$\Gamma_{ij} = \begin{cases} (1 + \exp\{-\gamma_{10} - \gamma_{11}x_{i1} - \sum_{h=2}^{r}\gamma_{1h}x_{ih}\})^{-1} & \text{if } j = 1, \\ \left(1 + \exp\{-\gamma_{j1}x_{i1} - \gamma_{j0} - \sum_{h=2}^{r}\gamma_{jh}x_{ih}\}\right)^{-1} & \text{if } j > 1, \end{cases}$$

where, for $j > 1$, Γ_{ij} is approximately equal to $\left(1 + \exp\{-2^j x_{i1}\}\right)^{-1}$ and, as $\gamma_{10} \to \infty$ and $\gamma_{11} \to -\infty$,

$$\Gamma_{i1} \to \begin{cases} 1 & \text{if } x_{i1} < \tilde{x}, \\ \varepsilon & \text{if } x_{i1} = \tilde{x}, \\ 0 & \text{if } x_{i1} > \tilde{x}, \end{cases}$$

where ε is small and close to zero. Notice that all entries are nonnegative, and all of the columns are linearly independent. Thus, over this region of the parameter space, $|\Gamma'\Gamma| > \delta > 0$ for some fixed $\delta > 0$. Since this region of the parameter space has infinite area, the integral of $|\Gamma'\Gamma|$ over the whole parameter space will be infinite. This same region of the parameter space also leads to strictly positive $|\mathbf{F}'\mathbf{F}|$ and $\begin{vmatrix} \mathbf{G}'\mathbf{G} & \mathbf{G}'\Gamma \\ \Gamma'\mathbf{G} & \Gamma'\Gamma \end{vmatrix}$. One can also find ranges of $\boldsymbol{\beta}$ so that the likelihood is larger than some positive constant over this same region of the $\boldsymbol{\gamma}$ parameter space. Thus the posterior will also be improper, for both the Jeffreys-rule prior and the independence Jeffreys prior. As with the flat prior, this can be worked around by suitably truncating the parameter space.

3.3.3   Reference Priors

Another approach to choosing a noninformative prior is to create one that lets the data have maximal influence on the posterior. Bernardo (1979) introduced a class of priors he called *reference priors*, which are chosen to do exactly this, for a particular definition of influence which is based on the change in information as measured by a variant of the Shannon information. Another important idea is to separate the parameters into separate classes of "parameters of interest" and "nuisance parameters" so that the goal is to maximize the effect of the data on the parameters of interest. Berger and Bernardo (1992) provide a more up-to-date discussion of reference priors, along with details on the construction of these priors, and some comparison with alternatives. Because Berger and Bernardo have published a number of papers on this topic, these priors are sometimes referred to as "Berger–Bernardo priors."

   Unfortunately, attempts to use the standard techniques to compute a reference prior for a neural network result in an improper prior that produces an improper posterior. Appendix A contains details on such a calculation. The posterior from this reference prior can be made proper by truncation, as with the other noninformative priors in this section.

3.4   Hybrid Priors

Some of the proposed priors combine elements of proper priors and noninformative priors. A basic prior for a neural network would be to combine the noninformative priors for $\boldsymbol{\beta}$ and σ^2 with independent normal priors for each γ_{jh}, i.e.,

$$P(\boldsymbol{\beta}) \propto 1,$$

$$P(\sigma^2) \propto \frac{1}{\sigma^2},$$

$$P(\gamma_{jh}) \sim N(0, v), \qquad j = 1, \ldots, k \ \ h = 0, \ldots, r,$$

which gives a proper posterior (unlike the unmodified priors of the previous section). This prior is notable because it is equivalent to using *weight decay*, a popular (non-Bayesian) method in machine learning for reducing overfitting. The usual specification of weight decay is as penalized maximum likelihood, where there is a penalty of $\frac{\|\boldsymbol{\gamma}_j\|}{v}$ for each of the hidden nodes. Thus, instead of maximizing only the likelihood $f(\mathbf{y}|\boldsymbol{\theta})$, one might maximize $f(\mathbf{y}|\boldsymbol{\theta}) - \sum_j \sum_h \frac{\gamma_{jh}^2}{\nu}$, which results in shrinkage of the parameters toward zero. The β_j parameters could also be shrunk if desired. Of course, the choice of ν is important, and various rules of thumb have been developed. Just as with ridge regression, this penalized maximum likelihood approach is equivalent to using a simple prior in a Bayesian context. Shrinkage-inducing priors will be revisited in Section 4.1.5.

Robinson (2001a; 2001b) proposes priors for parsimony on an effective domain of interest. He starts with the basic weight decay prior above, adds one level of hierarchy, putting an inverse-gamma prior with parameters a and b on ν, and then notes that ν can be integrated out leaving the marginal prior distribution for $\boldsymbol{\gamma}_j$ as a multivariate t, i.e., $P(\boldsymbol{\gamma}_j) \propto \left(1 + \frac{1}{b}||\boldsymbol{\gamma}_j||^2\right)^{-(a+r)/2}$. Note that the input bias term γ_{j0} is treated separately and is not included in $\boldsymbol{\gamma}_j$. From here, the problem is reparameterized to

$$\mathbf{w}_j = \frac{1}{||\boldsymbol{\gamma}_j||}\boldsymbol{\gamma}_j, \quad \mu_j = \frac{-\gamma_{j0}}{||\boldsymbol{\gamma}_j||}, \quad \lambda_j^2 = \frac{1}{||\boldsymbol{\gamma}_j||^2}$$

so that $\Psi(\gamma_{j0} + \boldsymbol{\gamma}_j^t \mathbf{x}_i) = \Psi(\frac{\mathbf{w}_j^t \mathbf{x}_i - \mu_j}{\lambda_j})$, where Ψ is the logistic function and represents a hidden node basis function (see equation (2.7)). Parsimony is then imposed either through orthogonality or additivity. For orthogonality, the multivariate t prior is modified to

$$P_{orth}(\mathbf{w}_1, \ldots, \mathbf{w}_k) \propto \left(1 + \frac{1}{b}\frac{2}{k(k-1)}\sum_{i<j}|\mathbf{w}_i^t\mathbf{w}_j|\right)^{-\frac{k(a+r)}{2}},$$

which penalizes for large $\frac{2}{k(k-1)}\sum_{i<j}|\mathbf{w}_i^t\mathbf{w}_j|$, which represents the average absolute pairwise dot product. This penalty is minimized when the parameter vectors are mutually orthogonal, and thus all pairwise dot products are zero. The idea here is that in driving the γ_j vectors towards orthogonality, one hopes to reduce the number of terms needed to represent the effects of the explanatory variables.

For additivity, define $g(\mathbf{w_j}) = \sum_h |w_{jh}| - 1$ and then modify the prior to

$$P_{add}(\mathbf{w}_1, \ldots, \mathbf{w}_k) \propto \prod_{j=1}^{k}\left(1 + \frac{1}{b}g(\mathbf{w}_j)\right)^{-\frac{a+r}{2}},$$

which maximizes the penalty when the unit vector $\mathbf{w}_j$ has equal elements and minimizes the penalty when $\mathbf{w}_j$ contains one element equal to 1 and all other elements equal to 0. This minimum penalty model is an additive model, a special case of the GAM models in Section 2.1.1. In both the orthogonal and additive cases, the hyperparameters a and b specify the amount of penalization. The standard noninformative prior is used for $\boldsymbol{\beta}$ and σ^2. A further suggestion is to restrict the action to an effective domain of interest, based on standardizing the covariates, centering the parameters, and using the correlation matrix of the covariates. For more details, see Robinson (2001a).

MacKay (1992) takes somewhat of an empirical Bayes approach. He starts out with a simple two-stage hierarchical model:

$$y_i \sim N\left(\sum_{j=0}^{k} \beta_j \Psi(\boldsymbol{\gamma}_j^t \mathbf{x}_i), \frac{1}{\nu}\right), \quad i = 1, \ldots, N,$$

$$\beta_j \sim N\left(0, \frac{1}{\alpha_1}\right), \quad j = 0, \ldots, k,$$

$$\gamma_{jh} \sim N\left(0, \frac{1}{\alpha_2}\right), \quad j = 1, \ldots, k, \quad h = 1, \ldots, r,$$

$$\gamma_{j0} \sim N\left(0, \frac{1}{\alpha_3}\right), \quad j = 1, \ldots, k,$$

$$\alpha_m \propto 1, \qquad\qquad m = 1, 2, 3,$$

$$\nu \propto 1.$$

The idea is to express ignorance with the flat and improper priors at the top level. However, this would then result in an improper posterior. So MacKay uses the data to fix the values for these hyperparameters (α_m and ν) at their posterior modes. This approach is essentially using a data-dependent prior for a one-stage model and represents a slightly different approach to get around putting too much information in the prior for parameters that do not have straightforward interpretations.

3.5   Model Fitting

At this point, we consider an important implementation issue—how to fit the model. Most of the literature on parameter estimation is from a classical viewpoint and is thus concerned only with finding a single best fit (e.g., maximum likelihood). This is typically done with a gradient descent technique. In particular, *backpropagation* (see, for example, Rumel-hart, Hinton, and Williams (1986)) makes use of the fact that the partial derivatives of the likelihood can be written in terms of the current estimates of the parameters and the current outputs of each layer, and can be done sequentially from the fitted values backwards through the layers of parameters. It is a computationally efficient algorithm, but it is merely a clever implementation of steepest descent. Many modifications to this algorithm have been proposed. The parameter estimation problem can also be viewed in the more general context of an optimization problem, and standard techniques such as quasi-Newton methods or simulated annealing can be applied. Ripley (1996) provides a thorough discussion of optimization techniques in the context of neural networks. It should also be noted that the likelihood is typically highly multimodal, and some care should be taken to ensure convergence to a global maximum (or typically to one of many symmetric global maxima, as the hidden node indices can be permuted without affecting the value of the likelihood).

From a Bayesian perspective, we want to estimate a posterior distribution. Sometimes we may want to attempt to describe the entire distribution. For that goal, we basically need to rely on Markov chain Monte Carlo, as described below. In other cases, we may only be interested in a point estimate, such as the posterior mode. In that case, we are in an analogous situation to the classical approach, and we have an optimization problem, although in this case the inclusion of the prior will generally destroy the elegant apparatus of backpropagation (unless the flat prior is used). It is then best to turn to quasi-Newton methods or other well-established numerical optimization routines.

In theory, the full posterior is given by Bayes' rule and is proportional to the likelihood multiplied by the prior. In some specific cases, the use of conjugate priors allows closed-form solutions for the posterior. In most problems, the posterior cannot be written in closed form because its normalizing constant involves an intractable integral. For a neural network, there is no known conjugate prior for the γ parameters inside of the logistic functions. We must then turn to approximation techniques, either analytical or numerical. An early Bayesian approach to the neural network problem was to first use backpropagation to get the maximum likelihood estimate (MLE) and then use a Gaussian approximation based at the MLE to estimate the full posterior (Buntine and Weigend (1991)). The current standard is to use the numerical simulation technique of Markov chain Monte Carlo (MCMC) for most Bayesian problems that cannot be done analytically, including neural networks.

MCMC works by drawing a sample from the posterior distribution. This sample can then be used empirically to estimate any aspect of the posterior such as its mean, variance, or distribution function. The sample can also be used to estimate derived distributions, such as posterior predictive distributions. Extended resources on MCMC are available (Robert and Casella (2000); Gilks, Richardson, and Spiegelhalter (1996); Gelman et al. (1995)). The "Markov chain" part of MCMC is in the drawing of the samples. The algorithm samples a Markov chain whose stationary distribution is the posterior distribution of interest. This is done by cleverly choosing the transition probabilities between steps and can be done without knowing the normalizing constant of the distribution, hence its great importance to practical Bayesian statistics. These transition probabilities are set up as one of two types of steps: Metropolis–Hastings (Metropolis et al. (1953); Hastings (1970)) or Gibbs (Geman and Geman (1984)) (although a Gibbs step is really a special case of a Metropolis step). At each step, a single (possibly multivariate) parameter, θ_n, is updated to θ_{n+1} by taking a step of the Markov chain while holding the other parameters fixed. Each of the other parameters is then cycled through and updated in turn.

For these updates, Metropolis–Hastings steps can always be used and consist of proposing a new value θ^* chosen randomly from the distribution $q(\theta^*|\theta_n)$ (which can depend on the current value θ_n) and either accepting this new value with probability $\alpha = \min(1, \frac{f(\mathbf{X}|\theta^*)P(\theta^*)q(\theta_n|\theta^*)}{f(\mathbf{X}|\theta_n)P(\theta_n)q(\theta^*|\theta_n)})$ or rejecting it and staying at the current value, i.e.,

$$\theta_{n+1} = \begin{cases} \theta^* & \text{with probability } \alpha, \\ \theta_n & \text{with probability } 1 - \alpha \ . \end{cases}$$

The acceptance probability is the ratio of the posterior evaluated at the new proposed value and the current value, adjusted by the probability of proposing that value if an asymmetric proposal distribution q is used. Note that since we are only concerned with a ratio of the posteriors, we do not need to know the normalizing constant, just the likelihood and the prior.

In some cases, this step can be simplified to a procedure known as Gibbs sampling. A useful concept is the complete conditional distribution for a parameter, also known as the full conditional distribution, which is the posterior distribution for that parameter when all other parameters are conditioned upon (held fixed). In some cases, the complete conditional distribution is a recognizable distribution from which samples can be easily drawn. For example, in linear regression, if the prior for the regression coefficients is either flat or normal, then the posterior distribution for the coefficients, when the variance is held fixed (conditioned on), is multivariate normal. In this case, an MCMC step can be conducted by drawing from this complete conditional distribution. One can think of this as using the complete conditional distribution as the sampling distribution q for a Metropolis–Hastings step, and then the acceptance probability $\alpha = 1$ because $q(\theta^*|\theta_n) = f(\mathbf{X}|\theta^*)P(\theta^*)$. Since the proposal is always accepted, the chain generally explores the parameter space much more efficiently than under standard Metropolis–Hastings. As a Gibbs step can be thought of as a special case of Metropolis–Hastings, both types of steps can be mixed together within a chain if some parameters have tractable complete conditionals and some do not, as is the case for a neural network. Conjugate and conditionally conjugate priors generally permit the use of Gibbs steps for those parameters.

For a neural network model, most standard choices of priors will lead to complete conditional distributions for $\boldsymbol{\beta}$ and σ^2 that are multivariate normal and inverse-gamma, respectively. Thus Gibbs steps can be used for both of these parameters. Unfortunately, there is no known prior that will allow the use of Gibbs sampling for $\boldsymbol{\gamma}$, so the γ_{jh} parameters must be updated with Metropolis–Hastings, either individually or in groups. One useful trick is to integrate out $\boldsymbol{\beta}$ when considering an update for γ_{jh}. Since the complete conditional distribution of $\boldsymbol{\beta}$ is multivariate normal, it is straightforward to complete the (multivariate) square and integrate it out. Using the marginal distribution for γ_{jh} allows the chain to move more freely, more efficiently exploring that part of the parameter space. If there are additional hyperparameters (such as in the models of Section 3.2), these can usually be updated with Gibbs steps.

To be more concrete, the steps for MCMC when using the flat prior of Section 3.3.1 are presented here. The following is easily modified for use with other priors. First, we write out the full posterior (without its intractable normalizing constant):

$$f(\boldsymbol{\gamma}, \boldsymbol{\beta}, \sigma^2|\mathbf{y}) \propto \frac{1}{\sigma^2}(2\pi\sigma^2)^{-n/2}\exp\left[-\frac{1}{2\sigma^2}(\mathbf{Z}\boldsymbol{\beta} - \mathbf{y})^t(\mathbf{Z}\boldsymbol{\beta} - \mathbf{y})\right]I_{\{\theta \in \Omega\}},$$

where $\mathbf{Z}$ is the matrix with elements $z_{ij} = \left[1 + \exp\left(-\gamma_{j0} - \sum_{h=1}^{r}\gamma_{jh}x_{ih}\right)\right]^{-1}$ as before, and Ω is a restriction of the parameter space as described after equation (3.2), for example, $\Omega = \{(\boldsymbol{\gamma}, \boldsymbol{\beta}, \sigma^2) : |\mathbf{Z}^t\mathbf{Z}| > 0.0001 \text{ and } |\gamma_{jh}| < 100,000 \text{ for all } j, h\}$. (Of course, other thresholds could be used, as long as the tails of the distribution are suitably truncated without affecting the range of possible fitted functions, as discussed in the paragraph just before equation (3.2).) The complete conditional distributions for $\boldsymbol{\beta}$ and σ^2 are normal and inverse-gamma, respectively:

$$\boldsymbol{\beta}|\boldsymbol{\gamma}, \sigma^2, \mathbf{y} \sim N\left((\mathbf{Z}^t\mathbf{Z})^{-1}\mathbf{Z}^t\mathbf{y}, (\mathbf{Z}^t\mathbf{Z})^{-1}\sigma^2\right), \tag{3.9}$$

$$\sigma^2|\boldsymbol{\gamma}, \mathbf{y} \sim \Gamma^{-1}\left(\frac{n-k-1}{2}, \frac{1}{2}\mathbf{y}^t(\mathbf{I} - \mathbf{Z}(\mathbf{Z}^t\mathbf{Z})^{-1}\mathbf{Z}^t)\mathbf{y}\right). \tag{3.10}$$

Note that $\mathbf{Z}(\mathbf{Z}^t\mathbf{Z})^{-1}\mathbf{Z}^t\mathbf{y}$ is the vector of fitted coefficients from a least-squares regression of $\mathbf{y}$ on $\mathbf{Z}$, and $\mathbf{y}^t(\mathbf{I} - \mathbf{Z}(\mathbf{Z}^t\mathbf{Z})^{-1}\mathbf{Z}^t)\mathbf{y} = \sum_{i=1}^{n}(y_i - \hat{y}_i)^2$ is the residual sum of squares for the least-squares estimates. The final calculation we need is the marginal posterior for $\boldsymbol{\gamma}$ after $\boldsymbol{\beta}$ and σ^2 have been integrated out:

$$f(\boldsymbol{\gamma}|\mathbf{y}) \propto |\mathbf{Z}^t\mathbf{Z}|^{-1/2} \left(\mathbf{y}^t(\mathbf{I} - \mathbf{Z}(\mathbf{Z}^t\mathbf{Z})^{-1}\mathbf{Z}^t)\mathbf{y}\right)^{-(n-k-1)/2} . \qquad (3.11)$$

Let $\boldsymbol{\gamma}_j = (\gamma_{j0}, \ldots, \gamma_{jr})$ be the vector of γ_{jh} associated with the jth hidden node (logistic basis function). An example MCMC algorithm which uses a multivariate Metropolis–Hastings draw for $\boldsymbol{\gamma}_j$ is as follows:

1. Start with arbitrary initial values for $\boldsymbol{\gamma}$ (making sure that $\boldsymbol{\gamma} \in \boldsymbol{\Omega}$).

2. Compute $\mathbf{Z}$.

3. Draw σ^2 via equation (3.10).

4. Draw $\boldsymbol{\beta}$ via equation (3.9).

5. For each j from $1, \ldots, k$, do the following Metropolis–Hastings step:

   (a) Generate a candidate $\boldsymbol{\gamma}_j^* \sim N(\boldsymbol{\gamma}_j, 0.05^2\mathbf{I})$.

   (b) Recompute Z with $\boldsymbol{\gamma}_j^*$ and compute $|\mathbf{Z}^t\mathbf{Z}|$.

   (c) If $|\mathbf{Z}^t\mathbf{Z}| > 0.0001$ and $|\gamma_{jh}| < 100,000$ for all j, h, accept $\boldsymbol{\gamma}_j^*$ with probability $\min(1, \frac{f(\boldsymbol{\gamma}^*|\mathbf{y})}{f(\boldsymbol{\gamma}|\mathbf{y})})$ computed from equation (3.11); otherwise, reject the candidate and keep the current value of γ_j.

6. Repeat steps 2 though 5 for the required number of iterations.

In step 5(a), the 0.05 in the proposal function should be treated as a tuning parameter and should be adjusted so that the acceptance probability is approximately 40%.

Some diagnostic tools are available to attempt to check for lack of convergence of the Markov chain. Typically the initial values from the chain (the burn-in iterations) are discarded, and only those believed to be from the stationary distribution are used for posterior calculations. The reader is referred to Gilks, Richardson, and Spiegelhalter (1996) for further discussion of convergence, examples, and additional references.

More sophisticated methods of generating proposals have been explored, such as hybrid Monte Carlo (Neal (1996)). In some cases, such algorithms can greatly improve the mixing of the chain. In practice, one must balance the gain in run time with the extra effort in programming and debugging time. Whether or not there is a net gain will be problem and programmer dependent.

3.6 Example Comparing Priors

To give some idea of the differences between the priors introduced in this chapter, Figure 3.6 shows the posterior means for fitting ozone levels from day of the year for a variety of choices of prior. Included are the proper priors of Müller and Rios Insua and of Neal, three noninformative priors (flat, independence Jeffreys, and reference), and the hybrid weight decay prior. The Neal and weight decay priors have user-specified hyperparameters that

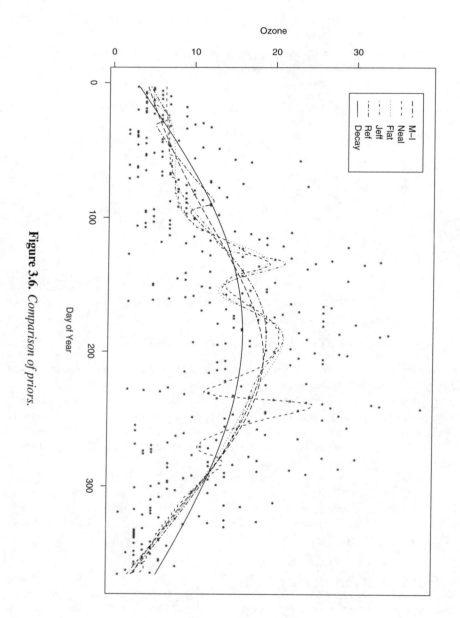

Figure 3.6. *Comparison of priors.*

greatly affect the behavior of the resulting posteriors, and values were picked here just as examples. The suggested default levels of Müller and Rios Insua were used, and the noninformative priors do not have user-specified hyperparameters.

Figure 3.6 shows that the posterior mean fit can have a wide variety of behaviors depending on the choice of prior. This weight decay prior produces the most shrinkage, resulting in a very smooth posterior mean. The Müller and Rios Insua is also highly informative and results in a smooth fit. In contrast, the other priors result in posterior means with more features that try to capture more of the variability in the data.

It is important to note that the weight decay and Neal priors can be adjusted by using different choices of hyperparameters. The examples provided here are meant to show a large part of the range of their flexibility. The weight decay prior has limiting cases with full shrinkage (the posterior mean is just a constant at the mean of the data) and no shrinkage (equivalent to the flat prior). The pictured plot shows a large amount of shrinkage (a more informative prior). The Neal prior similarly has a wide range, with the pictured plot representing very little shrinkage, but it could also be tuned to produce a large amount of shrinkage.

3.7   Asymptotic Consistency of the Posterior

Neural networks are able to approximate (Cybenko (1989); Funahashi (1989); Hornik, Stinchcombe, and White (1989)) a variety of functions (including any continuous function) with arbitrary accuracy. This section presents several results on the asymptotic properties of the posterior distribution for a neural network model. Starting with the assumption that there exists a "true" regression function, neighborhoods of this function will have posterior probability tending to one as the sample size grows arbitrarily large. The mean square error of the posterior predictive function also goes to zero in probability. This makes the somewhat frequentist assumption of a "true" regression function. However, it is useful to show that a Bayesian technique has good frequentist properties. First, a frequentist interested in better measures of uncertainty can use this Bayesian method as an approximation to frequentist methods. Second, the Bayesian method can be used by a Bayesian who wants to present the results to a non-Bayesian audience. Finally, a pure Bayesian will be interested to know that the method is asymptotically guaranteed to produce a reasonable answer when one exists.

The results in this section are from Lee (2000). Two approaches to consistency are taken. First is a sieve approach, where the number of hidden nodes increases as the sample size increases. Later, the number of hidden nodes is treated as a parameter.

A sieve is a series of models which grow with the sample size so that in the limit, the sieve will be wide enough to encompass models arbitrarily close to the true model (Grenander (1981); Wong and Shen (1995)). In this case, the number of hidden nodes is allowed to grow as a function of the sample size. The posterior can then be shown to be consistent over Hellinger neighborhoods (defined in equation (3.12) below), and the predictive regression function can be shown to be consistent. Some notation will allow a more precise statement of consistency. Denoting the explanatory variables as x and the response variable as y, let $f(x, y)$ be their joint density function, and let $f(y|x)$ be the corresponding regression function for y on x. Notationally, we distinguish dummy arguments x and y (lowercase) from theoretical random values X and Y (capital) and from observed data $\mathbf{X}$ and $\mathbf{Y}$ (capital and boldface). Denote the true function as f_0. Define a family of neighborhoods using the Hellinger distance by

$$A_\epsilon = \{f; D_H(f, f_0) \le \epsilon\}, \quad D_H(f, f_0) = \sqrt{\int\int \left(\sqrt{f(x, y)} - \sqrt{f_0(x, y)}\right)^2 dxdy}.$$

(3.12)

Let the number of hidden nodes in the model, k, grow with the sample size, n, such that $k_n \le n^a$ for any $0 < a < 1$. Let $\mathcal{F}_n$ be the set of all neural networks with each parameter less than C_n in absolute value, where C_n grows with n such that $C_n \le \exp(n^{b-a})$ for any constant b such that $0 < a < b < 1$ with the a from the bound for k_n. For any $\delta > 0$, denote the Kullback–Leibler neighborhood of f_0 of size δ by

$$K_\delta = \left\{f; E\left[\log \frac{f_0(x, y)}{f(x, y)}\right] \le \delta\right\}.$$

Denote the prior for f by $P_n(\cdot)$ and the posterior by $P(\cdot|\mathbf{X}, \mathbf{Y})$. Denote the predictive density by

$$\hat{f}_n(\cdot) = \int f(\cdot)dP(f|\mathbf{X}, \mathbf{Y}).$$

The predictive density is the Bayes estimate of f. The key result is the following theorem.

Theorem 3.1. *Suppose that* (i) *there exists a* $t > 0$ *and an* N_1 *such that* $P_n(\mathcal{F}_n^c) < \exp(-nt)$ *for all* $n \ge N_1$; (ii) *for all* $\delta, t > 0$, *there exists an* N_2 *such that* $P_n(K_\delta) \ge \exp(-nt)$ *for all* $n \ge N_2$. *Then for all* $\epsilon > 0$, *the posterior is asymptotically consistent for* f_0 *over Hellinger neighborhoods, i.e.,*

$$P(A_\epsilon|\mathbf{X}, \mathbf{Y}) \overset{P}{\to} 1.$$

(3.13)

Corollary 3.2. *Let* $g_0(x) = E_{f_0}[Y|X = x]$ *be the true regression function, and let* $\hat{g}_n(x) = E_{\hat{f}_n}[Y|X = x]$ *be the regression function from the predictive density using a neural network. Then, under the conditions of Theorem 3.1,* $\hat{g}_n$ *is asymptotically consistent for* g_0, *i.e.,*

$$\int (\hat{g}_n(x) - g_0(x))^2 dx \overset{P}{\to} 0.$$

(3.14)

The idea of the proof is to use bracketing entropy results from empirical process theory to bound the posterior probability outside the Hellinger neighborhoods of equation (3.12). The full proof (it is not short) can be found in Lee (2000), which follows the ideas of Barron, Schervish, and Wasserman (1999). The conditions of the theorem can be shown to hold for many standard choices of priors, such as those in Sections 3.2 and 3.3.

Instead of allowing the number of hidden nodes, k, to increase as a function of n, one can treat k as another parameter in the model and specify a prior for it. This approach also leads to an asymptotically consistent posterior. Let $\lambda_i = P(k = i)$ be the prior probability that the number of hidden nodes is i, $\sum \lambda_i = 1$. Let P_i be the prior for the parameters of the regression equation, given that $k = i$. The joint prior for all of the parameters is $\sum_i \lambda_i P_i$. One can now extend the result of Theorem 3.1.

Theorem 3.3. *Suppose that* (i) *there exists a sequence $t_i > 0$ and a sequence N_i such that for each i, $P_i(\mathcal{F}_n^c) < \exp(-nt_i)$ for all $n \geq N_i$;* (ii) *for all $\delta, t > 0$, there exists an I and a sequence M_i such that for any $i \geq I$, $P_i(K_\delta) \geq \exp(-nt)$ for all $n \geq M_i$;* (iii) B_n *is a bound which grows with n such that for all $t > 0$, there exists a $q > 1$ and an N such that $\sum_{i=B_n+1}^{\infty} \lambda_i < \exp(-n^q t)$ for $n \geq N$;* (iv) *for all i, $\lambda_i > 0$. Then for all $\epsilon > 0$,*

$$P(A_\epsilon | \mathbf{X}, \mathbf{Y}) \xrightarrow{P} 1. \tag{3.15}$$

Again, the proof can be found in Lee (2000). The conditions on the prior for k hold for most standard choices of priors, including geometric and Poisson distributions. One can also draw analogous conclusions to Corollary 3.2, in that the mean square error of the predictive regression function goes to zero in probability.

Chapter 4

Building a Model

It is insufficient to pick an arbitrary number of logistic basis functions, pick a prior, fit the model using all of the available explanatory variables, and assume that everything will work out fine. The key question is, "Is this the right model?" This chapter looks at issues in building a model, first addressing issues and methodology related to choosing a model and then examining how one might do this in practice when faced with a dauntingly large model space.

4.1 Model Selection and Model Averaging

Nearly all statistical problems are faced with a trade-off between fitting and overfitting. Overfitting occurs when the model is made to match a particular dataset too closely. Most data contain a certain amount of noise or inherent randomness. If a model is made to fit too well, it will model not just the underlying trend but also model the noise. Fitting the noise is bad not only from a pedagogical viewpoint but also from a theoretical one, in that predictive accuracy will decrease as overfitting increases. As an extreme example, suppose one wants to model the probability that it rains tomorrow, and data is collected for a week by each day flipping a fair coin ten times, recording the number of heads, and then recording whether or not it rains the next day. It is likely that a complex enough model, such as a neural network with a large number of nodes, can find a good fit between the number of heads one day and the presence of rain on the next. Obviously, this model will be useless in practice, as its chance of predicting rain will be no more accurate than a model containing only an intercept term (i.e., predicting the probability that it rains tomorrow to be the probability that it rained on any given day of the data collection period, ignoring any possible covariates). Not only is there no gain in accuracy, but there is also a large increase in predictive variability, as the model attempts to predict different probabilities based on the coins. This increased variability means the mean square error of prediction is larger than if we fit a model without this extraneous variable. Thus the goal of modeling is to find the most appropriate model, fitting as well as possible without overfitting.

In the context of neural networks, there are two key areas for model selection: the choice of explanatory variables and the number of basis functions. Not all variables are as

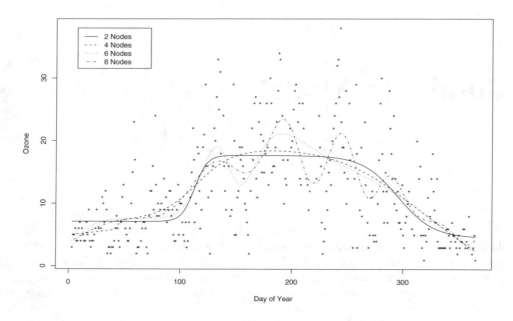

Figure 4.1. *Fitted mean functions for several sizes of networks.*

obviously irrelevant as the number of heads on ten flips of a fair coin, but ones which do
not sufficiently contribute to the model should be excluded. Multicollinearity (correlation
between explanatory variables) can also lead to predictive instability, and model selection
can help reduce predictive mean square error in this situation.

The second concern is the number of logistic basis functions. A smaller number means
a smoother fitted function, while a larger number can model more complex relationships
but can be prone to overfitting if too many hidden nodes are used. Figure 4.1 shows the
posterior mean fitted functions for predicting ozone levels from the day of the year for neural
networks with two, four, six, and eight hidden nodes when the flat prior (equation (3.2))
is used. The fits with two and four basis functions are relatively smooth and capture the
main shape of of data. With six basis functions, one starts to see additional features to the
fit. With eight basis functions, the fit becomes much more variable, appearing to overfit
considering the large amount of noise in the data (the scatter from the fit in both directions).
Thus it is necessary to tune the model to use the optimal number of basis functions. The
rest of this section will investigate a number of issues and approaches for dealing with one
or both aspects of neural network model selection.

Sample size can also affect model building. With smaller sample sizes, it can be difficult to distinguish between a true signal and noise, making both overfitting and underfitting
highly problematic. Larger sample sizes generally allow better estimation of the magnitude
of the error, and thus separating the underlying function from the noise can be more straightforward. However, there is often the tendency to include more parameters as the sample

size increases, thus allowing overfitting on a finer scale. As neural networks are complex and nonintuitive creatures, there are no rules of thumb for ratios of sample size to number of parameters. Practitioners are urged to use their judgment and be wary of overfitting.

4.1.1 Modeling Versus Prediction

There are two main reasons for doing model selection—improving predictions and model selection for its own sake. In much of statistics (and virtually all of machine learning), the focus is on prediction. A model is merely a tool for producing good predictions. In some cases, it may be assumed that there is a correct underlying model, while in others it may not. In both cases, the fitted model is usually viewed only as a "best approximation" with the realization that the emphasis is on being able to make useful predictions. For example, the ozone dataset introduced in Section 1.3 is a case where our primary interest is being able to predict future ozone levels (from meteorological data). The need for model selection or other shrinkage methods stems from a desire for good predictions. The fact that some of the covariates are highly correlated makes model selection a good choice for reducing predictive variability. But the focus is not on pure model selection, as it is in the next paragraph.

A contrasting situation is one where there is a substantive reason to actually want to choose between two or more models for scientific or practical reasons. There may be a philosophical reason to believe that there is a true model, and thus the goal of a statistical analysis is to determine which model is most likely to be the truth. For example, some ecologists believe that there exists a model which determines the movements of manatee populations, but there is disagreement over exactly what this model is and which covariates are in it. Statisticians have been called in to help choose among competing models (Craig (1997)). A different situation requiring model selection is the choosing of variables for economic reasons. There are a number of examples of the need to sort through a large number of variables and only retain a relatively small number. One such example is a study that will be done in stages where a pilot study will collect data on many possible explanatory variables, but only a small selection of these will be used for the full study because of funding constraints. Another example is the loan applications dataset introduced in Section 1.4, where the bank wanted to simplify the application form, both to make the process more customer friendly, as well as to streamline operations and save money for the bank. In these cases, it is important not only to find a model that fits well but also to find one that uses only as many explanatory variables as is absolutely necessary.

Depending on the motivation for model selection (prediction vs. pure model selection), different tools may be appropriate. When prediction is the goal, approaches that produce shrinkage (such as weight decay or proper priors; see Section 4.1.5) will automatically down-weight less important variables and reduce predictive variability. However, such methods would not be helpful for pure model selection, since all variables are retained even though the effective dimension is reduced. If a shrinkage prior were used in the examples in the previous paragraph, the collaborating scientist would not be able to cleanly choose between competing models, and the bank in question would not be able to easily eliminate variables. Variables with small coefficients could be dropped, but there are no theoretical results to guide the choice of threshold for dropping a variable. Another potential problem is the case of two highly correlated variables where shrinkage causes one of the two to be the primary variable in one basis function but the other one to be the main effect in a different basis function. Since they each are important in different nodes, neither could obviously be dropped from the model. In the rest of this chapter, a variety of approaches will be presented, some primarily useful for prediction, others useful for both prediction and pure model selection.

4.1.2   Bayesian Model Selection

In principle, model selection under the Bayesian approach is straightforward. The choice of model can be considered a hyperparameter, with the prior distributions of the model parameters dependent on the choice of model (usually these conditional priors will be the same across all models that include that parameter, but some models will have fewer or different parameters than others). In practice, this means a prior $P(M_i)$ must be chosen for the space $\mathcal{M}$ of possible models M_i, and the posterior probabilities of the models are found via Bayes' theorem:

$$P(M_i|\mathbf{y}) = \frac{P(\mathbf{y}|M_i)P(M_i)}{\sum_{M_j \in \mathcal{M}} P(\mathbf{y}|M_j)P(M_j)} , \tag{4.1}$$

where $P(\mathbf{y}|M_i)$ is the marginal probability of the data under model M_i with the parameters integrated out, i.e.,

$$P(\mathbf{y}|M_i) = \int f(\mathbf{y}|\boldsymbol{\theta}, M_i)P(\boldsymbol{\theta}|M_i)\,d\boldsymbol{\theta} , \tag{4.2}$$

where $f(\mathbf{y}|\boldsymbol{\theta}, M_i)$ is the likelihood under model M_i and $P(\boldsymbol{\theta}|M_i)$ is the prior distribution of the parameters under model M_i. Note that $P(\mathbf{y}|M_i)$ is the normalizing constant for the posterior distribution of the parameters of model M_i (which may be not be computable in closed form for some models).

Instead of posterior probabilities of models, sometimes the comparison is done using *Bayes factors*. The Bayes factor for comparing two models is the ratio of the posterior odds in favor of the first model to the prior odds in favor of the first; i.e., the Bayes factor for comparing model i to model j is

$$B_{ij} = \frac{\frac{P(M_i|\mathbf{y})}{P(M_j|\mathbf{y})}}{\frac{P(M_i)}{P(M_j)}} = \frac{P(\mathbf{y}|M_i)}{P(\mathbf{y}|M_j)} .$$

So, once again, we need to compute the marginal probabilities of the data under the different models. Kass and Raftery (1995) provide a review of Bayes factors in the context of model selection.

One important technical note is that since we are looking at the normalizing constant for the posterior of the parameters of a model, this term will depend on the normalizing constant of the prior for the parameters. When an improper prior (such as $P(\beta) \propto 1$) is used, it does not usually matter what constant is in front. However, this constant does figure into the posterior probability for model selection, so a particular constant must be chosen when model selection is being done. If the constant depends on the dimension of the model (number of parameters), as it often does (e.g., the power of the 2π term for a multivariate normal), then it is critical for model selection that this term be explicitly included. Efforts to define Bayes factors that avoid the problem of arbitrary constants with improper priors include fractional Bayes factors (O'Hagan (1995)) and intrinsic Bayes factors (Berger and Pericchi (1996)). Obviously, this is not an issue for proper priors, as their normalizing constants are uniquely specified.

A key element of model probabilities is the specification of prior probabilities for the models, $P(M_j)$, in equation (4.1). In the absence of any prior information, a convenient choice is to set all models under consideration to be equal, a discrete uniform distribution. For a neural network, this is equivalent to having the probability of inclusion of each explanatory variable be independent and equal to 1/2, and independently have a discrete uniform distribution on the number of hidden nodes (typically restricted to some fixed range). Choices of priors for the models can have both obvious and unexpected ramifications on the posterior distribution (for example, see Clyde (1999) and the accompanying discussion). This book uses the uniform prior described above, but the methods are easily adapted to any other prior.

Once the posterior probabilities of the different models are computed, it is trivial to pick a "best" model by choosing the one with highest posterior probability. In some cases, one may want to ask if a particular explanatory variable is important, and the marginal posterior probability of importance of that variable can be computed by summing the posterior probabilities of all models that include that variable. An alternative to the highest posterior probability model is the median probability model, that which includes all covariates that have marginal probability of at least 1/2 being included in the model and has been shown to be optimal for prediction in linear regression in certain cases (Barbieri and Berger (2002)).

While this approach is great in theory, the marginal probability of the data, $P(\mathbf{y}|M_i)$, is an analytically intractable integral. In fact, this is exactly the integral that is avoided by using MCMC to estimate the posterior distribution of the parameters. In practice, we must resort to numerical approximations of this integral. Some methods are discussed in the next section.

4.1.3 Computational Approximations for Model Selection

To estimate a posterior probability, first the normalizing constant for the posterior of the parameters needs to be estimated. This turns out to be a very difficult problem in the case of a neural network. Methods for estimating normalizing constants can generally be classified into one of two types: numerical methods and posterior simulation-based methods. Numerical methods attempt to estimate the integral directly from the unnormalized function and include integration techniques such as quadrature and Monte Carlo integration. Posterior simulation-based methods use a sample from the posterior (such as an MCMC sample) and include Laplace approximation (Tierney and Kadane (1986)), importance sampling (Geweke (1989)), reciprocal importance sampling (Gelfand and Dey (1994)), and bridge sampling (Meng and Wong (1996)). A useful overview of estimation methods is Evans and Swartz (1995). A review of these methods applied to neural networks appears in Lee (2002). Additional discussion appears in French and Rios Insua (2000, Chapter 7). It turns out that none of them work well. What has been found to work best is something simpler, the Bayesian information criterion (BIC) (Schwarz (1978)) approximation. Originally developed as a model selection technique in response to the frequentist Akaike information criterion (AIC) (Akaike (1974)), the BIC is an approximation to the log of the Bayes factor for comparing a model to the null model (a regression model with only an intercept term or a classification model that predicts the probability of class membership to be the empirical marginal probabilities). The BIC of model i is defined as

$$BIC_i = f(\mathbf{y}|\hat{\boldsymbol{\theta}}, M_i) - \frac{1}{2}d_i \log n,$$

where $f(\mathbf{y}|\hat{\boldsymbol{\theta}}, M_i)$ is the maximum value of the likelihood of model i, d_i is the number of parameters in model i, and n is the sample size. Thus the BIC is a penalized likelihood criterion, as are the AIC and the network information criterion (NIC), which is meant to adjust the penalty for the number of parameters in a neural network because the parameters are not independent (Murata, Yoshizawa, and Amari (1994)). As the BIC is an approximation to the log of a Bayes factor, ratios of exponentiated BICs give approximate posterior probabilities. Denoting the null model by M_0 and assuming that all models have equal prior probability (otherwise another factor for the model priors needs to be included),

$$P(M_i|\mathbf{y}) = \frac{P(\mathbf{y}|M_i)}{\sum_j P(\mathbf{y}|M_j)} = \frac{\frac{P(\mathbf{y}|M_i)}{P(\mathbf{y}|M_0)}}{\sum_j \frac{P(\mathbf{y}|M_j)}{P(\mathbf{y}|M_0)}} = \frac{B_{i0}}{\sum_j B_{j0}} \approx \frac{e^{BIC_i}}{\sum_j e^{BIC_j}}. \qquad (4.3)$$

Technically, the asymptotic approximation is that $BIC_i = \log P(\mathbf{y}|M_i) + O_P(1)$ (see, for example, Kass and Wasserman (1995)). While the accuracy of this approximation may appear low, the BIC has been shown to be asymptotically consistent for model selection for many classes of models, including mixture models (Keribin (2000)), which share many similarities with neural networks. The BIC approximation has also been found to work well in practice (Lee (2002)). Typically the interest is in using the BIC for model selection, rather than for actual estimates of Bayes factors, and so the fact that it is a low-order approximation to the Bayes factor is less of an issue as long as it works well for the relative differences between models, which it usually does. The BIC also has the advantage of being quite simple to calculate, in that only the likelihood needs to be maximized, and there is much existing software for computing maximum likelihood estimates for neural network models; for example, code is available for S-PLUS (Venables and Ripley (1999)) and SAS (Sarle (1994)) among many others. This approximation eliminates the potential problem of having to run separate MCMC algorithms for many different possible models. The "best" model can be found by comparing BICs, and then a full MCMC can be run only on that model.

4.1.4 Model Averaging

In some cases, there will be more than one model with high posterior probability, and these models will give different predictions (see, for example, the heart attack data in Raftery (1996)). Using only a single model will then grossly underestimate the variability of the estimate, since it would ignore the fact that another model with significant posterior probability made a different prediction. Instead, one should calculate predictions (or statistics thereof) by using a weighted average over all models in the search space, where the weights are the posterior probabilities of the models (Leamer (1978); Kass and Raftery (1995); Draper (1995)). Let y^* be the response variable being predicted for possibly new values of the explanatory variables $\mathbf{x}^*$. Then the full posterior predictive distribution of y^*, taking into account model uncertainty, is

$$P(y^*|\mathbf{x}^*, \mathbf{y}, \mathbf{x}) = \sum_{M_i \in \mathcal{M}} P(y^*|\mathbf{x}^*, \mathbf{y}, \mathbf{x}, M_i) P(M_i|\mathbf{y}, \mathbf{x}),$$

where $P(y^*|\mathbf{x}^*, \mathbf{y}, \mathbf{x}, M_i) = \int P(y^*|\mathbf{x}^*, \boldsymbol{\theta}, M_i) P(\boldsymbol{\theta}|\mathbf{y}, \mathbf{x}, M_i) d\boldsymbol{\theta}$ is the marginal posterior predictive density given a particular model (with all other parameters integrated out), and $P(M_i|\mathbf{y}, \mathbf{x})$ is the posterior probability of model i (note that $\mathbf{x}^*$ and $\mathbf{x}$ are usually suppressed from the notation, as they are considered "fixed").

Thus model averaging produces the most complete accounting for uncertainty, by including uncertainty about the choice of model, an aspect often ignored in analyses. By using the full posterior, model averaging can also result in dramatic decreases in prediction errors (Raftery, Madigan, and Hoeting (1997)). A good review article on model averaging is Hoeting et al. (1999). Of course, if the posterior puts nearly all of its probability on a single model (which is not uncommon), using a single model and doing model averaging will produce essentially identical results, and so averaging is not necessary.

4.1.5 Shrinkage Priors

All proper priors produce shrinkage. But a prior can be chosen to specifically shrink towards parsimonious models, as an alternative to direct model selection. In the simplest case, this can be independent priors with mean zero for each parameter. When these priors are Gaussian, this is equivalent to using weight decay, as discussed in Section 3.4. This choice of prior shrinks the fitted coefficients towards zero, helping to avoid overfitting and improving predictions. Shrinkage priors are better suited for prediction than model selection, but model selection of a sort can be done by removing parameters that are close to zero. However, there are only ad hoc guidelines for deciding (i) how much shrinkage to use and (ii) what is considered "close to zero."

The parsimony priors of Robinson (2001a; 2001b) that were introduced in Section 3.4 are specifically designed to give higher posterior probability to simpler models, where "simple" is measured either through orthogonality or additivity. When using the orthogonality prior, prediction can be done effectively without worrying too hard about selecting covariates, as multicollinearity will be kept under control by the prior.

Neal's multilevel hierarchical prior (Neal (1996)), introduced in Section 3.2, is a more complex prior for shrinkage. The prior structure is flexible enough to produce different amounts of shrinkage for different parameters. Hyperparameters for unimportant covariates or basis functions will increase shrinkage on their coefficients, thus controlling overfitting.

4.1.6 Automatic Relevance Determination

The goal of automatic relevance determination (ARD) is to shrink the effect of covariates that are not actively contributing to the model, acting as a surrogate for model selection over the possible explanatory variables. Developed by MacKay (1994) and Neal (1996), the motivation was to improve prediction when faced with a large set of covariates. The idea is to include each possible covariate and to give it its own hyperparameter that affects the magnitude of all parameters relating to that covariate. A covariate that turns out to be unhelpful for prediction will then have the posterior for its hyperparameter concentrate on small values so that all of the γ_{jh}'s associated with that covariate will be shrunk toward zero. For example, suppose the original prior for γ_{jh} is $N(\mu_\gamma, \sigma_\gamma^2)$. Using ARD, the new prior would be $N(\mu_\gamma, \alpha_h \sigma_\gamma^2)$, where α_h is the new hyperparameter associated with the hth covariate. Each α_h would then be given its own prior distribution; in this case an inverse-gamma with prespecified shape and scale would be the most straightforward (as it is conditionally conjugate). If the posterior for α_h tends toward small values, then so will γ_{jh} for all j, and the impact of covariate h will be limited.

ARD can be viewed as a shrinkage prior that acts only on sets of possible covariates, rather than acting directly on the parameters as did the priors in the previous section. An ad hoc model selection technique can be derived from ARD, in that if the hyperparameter for a covariate is sufficiently close to zero, that covariate can be dropped from the model. This procedure is ad hoc, in that the choice of "sufficiently close to zero" is arbitrary. ARD has the advantage of being able to act on all possible covariates simultaneously, eliminating the difficulties of searching through the high-dimensional space of possible subsets covariates (an issue discussed further in Section 4.2). Another advantage of ARD is that it is straightforward to apply to many complex models such as neural networks, where more traditional methods have trouble dealing with the nonlinearities in the model. Neal (1996) demonstrates the efficacy of ARD for neural network models on several datasets.

4.1.7   Bagging

Bagging (Breiman (1996)) is an ensemble learning method that uses bootstrapping to attempt to reduce prediction variance (overfitting) while not oversmoothing (underfitting). The name bagging is short for "Bootstrap AGGregatING," which describes the procedure. Instead of using a single model to make predictions, bootstrap samples are taken from the original data, the model is fit on each sample, and predictions from each of these bootstrap replications are averaged to get the bagged prediction. To be more precise, denote the observed data by $X = (x_1, \ldots, x_n)$. Let $\mathbf{X_m}$ be a bootstrap sample of the data, i.e., a sample of size n taken from $\mathbf{X}$ with replacement, $X_m = (x_{m_1}, \ldots, x_{m_n})$, where $m_i \in \{1, \ldots, n\}$ with repetitions allowed. The sample $\mathbf{X_m}$ can also be thought of as a reweighted version of $\mathbf{X}$, where the weights, $\omega_i^{(m)}$, are drawn from the set $\{0, \frac{1}{n}, \frac{2}{n}, \ldots, 1\}$ and correspond to the number of times that x_i appears in the bootstrap sample. Suppose we want to predict (in either a regression or classification setting) the response variable for a particular value of the explanatory variables, $\mathbf{x_j}$. Let $G(\mathbf{x_j}|\mathbf{X_m})$ be the predicted values for inputs $\mathbf{x_j}$ from a neural network model trained on data $\mathbf{X_m}$. Let M be the number of bootstrap samples that are used. Then the bagging predictor for inputs $\mathbf{x_j}$ in a regression problem is $\frac{1}{M} \sum_{m=1}^M G(\mathbf{x_j}|\mathbf{X_m})$. For classification, the predicted category from bagging is the one that is most frequently predicted by $G(\mathbf{x_j}|\mathbf{X_1})_j, \ldots, G(\mathbf{x_j}|\mathbf{X_M})_j$. A pseudocode version of this algorithm for regression follows:

1. For $m \in \{1, \ldots, M\}$,

   (a) draw a bootstrap sample, $\mathbf{X_m}$, from $\mathbf{X}$;

   (b) find predicted values $G(\mathbf{x_j}|\mathbf{X_m})$.

2. The bagging predictor is $\frac{1}{M} \sum_{m=1}^{M} G(\mathbf{x_j}|\mathbf{X_m})$.

Breiman (1996) explains that bagging is most helpful for unstable modeling procedures, i.e., those for which the predictions are sensitive to small changes in the data. He also provides a theoretical explanation of how bagging works, demonstrating the reduction in mean-squared prediction error for unstable procedures. Breiman (1994) showed that neural networks, classification and regression trees, and model selection for regression are all unstable procedures. Bagging is sometimes described as a frequentist approximation to Bayesian model averaging, because it is averaging over multiple models. Bühlmann and Yu (2002) provide some theoretical analysis of how and why bagging works.

Bagging can be brought into the Bayesian paradigm by replacing the ordinary bootstrap with the Bayesian bootstrap (Rubin (1981)). The Bayesian bootstrap reweights the sample with continuous-valued weights, instead of restricting the weights to the set $\{0, \frac{1}{n}, \frac{2}{n}, \ldots, 1\}$. Treating the weights ω_i as unknown parameters, the noninformative prior $\prod_{i=1}^{n} \omega_i^{-1}$ combines with a multinomial likelihood to give a posterior distribution for $\boldsymbol{\omega}$ that is Dirichlet$(1, \ldots, 1)$. Then $E[\omega_i] = 1/n$ for all i, so the expected values of the weights are the same under the ordinary and Bayesian bootstraps. The correlation between the weights is also the same. The variance of the weights under the Bayesian bootstrap is $n/(n+1)$ that of the ordinary bootstrap, so for a linear functional of the weights (such as a linear regression or a CART model), bagging with the Bayesian bootstrap will have variability that is strictly less than that of ordinary bagging. Denote the reweighted dataset as $(X, \boldsymbol{\omega}^{(m)})$. Pseudocode for Bayesian bagging follows:

1. For $m \in \{1, \ldots, M\}$,

   (a) draw random weights $\boldsymbol{\omega}^{(m)}$ from a $Dirichlet_n(1, \ldots, 1)$ to produce the Bayesian bootstrap sample $(X, \boldsymbol{\omega}^{(m)})$;

   (b) find predicted values $G(\mathbf{x_j}|\mathbf{X}, \boldsymbol{\omega}^{(m)})$.

2. The bagging predictor is $\frac{1}{M} \sum_{m=1}^{M} G(\mathbf{x_j}|\mathbf{X}, \boldsymbol{\omega}^{(m)})$.

Further details on Bayesian bagging are available in Clyde and Lee (2001).

Since neural networks are unstable procedures (Breiman (1994)), they can benefit from bagging. A model can be fit with potentially extra hidden nodes or covariates, and bagging can be used to reduce the effect of overfitting.

For example, Figure 4.2 shows bagging in action. The five solid lines are posterior mean fits from five Bayesian bootstrap samples using a neural network with six basis functions and the usual flat prior (equation (3.2)). The dashed line is the bagged fit using 50 Bayesian bootstrap samples (the other 45 are not pictured for figure clarity). The bagged fit captures the main features of most of the individual fits, yet is smoother than most of them. Thus the fit is shrunk toward a less variable function by the aggregation, reducing the effect of overfitting seen by using six basis functions.

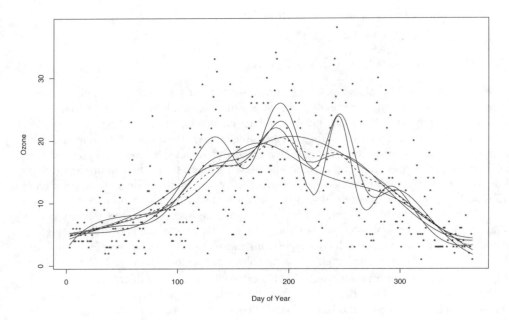

Figure 4.2. *Bagging example: The solid lines are fits from bootstrap samples and the dashed line is the bagged fit.*

4.2   Searching the Model Space

Model selection seeks the model with highest posterior probability. Model averaging requires finding all models with relatively high posterior probability. In both cases, one needs a way to explore the space of possible models in order to find the best models without doing an exhaustive search, which will typically be computationally prohibitive. Consider trying to find the best subset of r explanatory variables for a neural network with a fixed number of hidden nodes. There are 2^r possible models, which will quickly grow past a manageable size as r increases. If we also consider models with different numbers of hidden nodes, the search space is even larger. Note that the methods of Sections 4.1.5 through 4.1.7 are attempts to avoid this full model search. When it is infeasible to do an exhaustive search, posterior probabilities are estimated only for the set of models in the search path, and the probabilities of other models not visited is estimated to be small and therefore set to zero. The rest of this section will examine a number of different searching strategies. First up are greedy algorithms, which deterministically choose the best model under consideration at each step. Next are stochastic algorithms, ones which may choose randomly each step (but with weighted probabilities so that they tend to go in good directions). Last is a special stochastic algorithm, reversible jump Markov chain Monte Carlo, which uses MCMC to simultaneously estimate the joint posterior of the model space and the model parameters.

Before getting to the search strategies, let us consider the issue of fitting the parameters for a single model. All of the strategies other than reversible jump are iterative procedures that at each step compare a small number of possible models (often just two). To compare these models, an estimate of the posterior probabilities (equation (4.1)) of these models is needed. This requires fitting each of the models under consideration, either as a maximization (and using the BIC or another approximation from Section 4.1.3) or finding the full posterior via MCMC and marginalizing over the parameters. As a full MCMC is computationally expensive, when searching over large model spaces it is more practical to use a maximization approximation such as the BIC approximation for posterior probabilities (equation (4.3)), and then after the search is complete the best model or models can be returned to and will fit a full MCMC. That approach is taken in the rest of this section.

A final note about searching the model space needs to be made in the context of neural networks. In many statistical applications, one can fit the model analytically (e.g., linear regression) or numerically with reasonable confidence (e.g., logistic regression). However, fitting a neural network, in either a frequentist or Bayesian framework, involves the use of an iterative algorithm which could find a local maximum rather than a global maximum. When fitting models one at a time, the user can look at plots of fits and make a reasonable determination of whether the true maximum (or something quite close) has been found. However, when using an automated algorithm that will be fitting hundreds or thousands of models, it is not possible to check them all by hand. One should keep in mind that a model visited during a search algorithm may not necessarily be fit optimally. One idea that can help is to fit each model several times, starting the iterative fitting algorithm at several different places, and to use only the best fit found, which will more likely be the global maximum.

4.2.1 Greedy Algorithms

Stepwise algorithms for finding a best model have long existed in the linear regression literature, but they are widely applicable and can be adapted for use with neural networks. For linear regression, the basic idea is to move through the space of possible covariates by taking steps consisting of adding or deleting a single variable. At each step, the process can move forward (adding variables) or backward (removing variables). As a greedy algorithm, in forward mode it picks the single best variable to add at each step by maximizing some criterion (such as the BIC) over the possible models that would result from adding a variable. The algorithm continues moving in the same direction until no more variables can be added. The algorithm then reverses direction and attempts to remove variables. This process continues until the algorithm switches directions in two consecutive steps, indicating that no better models are one step away from the current model, or from any previous model visited, and so the algorithm ends. For a neural network model, adding or removing a single variable entails more than just one parameter, since a γ_{jh} is needed for each basis function. Also, the stepwise algorithm can be used to search over the number of basis functions in the network, with each forward step considering adding a hidden node and each backward step considering removing one. Pseudocode for a stepwise model search for a neural network follows:

1. Find the fit and BIC for the starting model (typically the null model with no hidden nodes or a model with many hidden nodes and all of the possible covariates).

2. Generate candidate models:

    (a) If moving forward, fit all of the models with one more covariate than the current model, as well as the model with one more hidden node than the current model.

    (b) If moving backward, fit all of the models with one less covariate than the current model, as well as the model with one less hidden node than the current model.

3. Compute the BICs for each of these candidate models. If any of the candidates has a BIC that is larger than the BIC of the current model, then choose the candidate model with the largest BIC and make that the new current model.

4. If a better candidate model was found, then return to step 2 and continue moving in the same direction.

5. If a better candidate model was not found (all candidate models had smaller BICs than the current model), then return to step 2 but switch directions.

6. If the direction is switched in two consecutive passes, then no better models exist with either one more or one less variable or node, so terminate the algorithm.

Note that it is usually computationally more efficient to keep track of the BICs for all models considered so that if they come up for consideration again, they do not need to be fit again. Stepwise algorithms are admittedly ad hoc and may not find the model with highest posterior probability. However, they often work well in practice and are relatively simple to implement, so they are worth trying. They tend to run into trouble when the effects of variables are correlated so that an important interaction between two variables may not be found when the algorithm is only allowed to move in steps of one variable at a time.

Stepwise algorithms are generally designed only to find a single best model. For model averaging, a set of best models is desired. Occam's Window (Raftery and Madigan (1994)) was designed with this goal in mind. It narrows the model space by keeping only models with high posterior probability relative to the set of models currently under consideration. In addition, the algorithm employs the principle of Occam's Razor, in that if two models have equal posterior probability, then the simpler model is to be preferred to the larger model. The details of which models are kept under consideration and which models are excluded from the final set of models follow:

1. Exclude from consideration any model with posterior probability less than $1/c$ times that of the model with highest posterior probability. $c = 20$ is suggested as a guideline, which is compared to the standard 0.05 cutoff for a p-value.

2. When comparing submodels of the current model, exclude all submodels of any submodels which have been excluded by the first rule.

3. When comparing supermodels of the current model, exclude all supermodels which do not have higher posterior probability than the current model.

Note that the log of the ratio of posterior probabilities can be approximated by a difference of BICs. Also note that stronger evidence is required to exclude a smaller model than is required to exclude a larger model. This asymmetry is due to the application of Occam's Razor.

Occam's Window is actually run as a pair of algorithms, once in an upward direction and once in a downward direction. These directions can be done in either order so that one can start with a small (or null) model, grow that model with the up algorithm to get a set of models under consideration, and then run the down algorithm on each of the models found from the up algorithm to get a final set of models. Or the algorithm could start with a large model on which the down algorithm is run. The subset of models found by the down algorithm would then be fed into the up algorithm to find the final set of models with high posterior probability. This algorithm has similar problems as the stepwise algorithm. First, it may become stuck in local maxima of the model space because it considers only local moves in a greedy fashion. Second, when fitting a candidate model, one does not know if the maximization algorithm has actually found the global maximum, so a poor convergence in the fitting algorithm could irrevocably steer Occam's Window down the wrong path in the model space. Fitting each candidate model multiple times and using the fit with the best BIC when deciding if the model should be kept or excluded can help with this second problem.

4.2.2   Stochastic Algorithms

Stochastic searching algorithms attempt to avoid becoming stuck in local maxima of the model space by introducing some randomness into the search. The trade-off is that they are more computationally intensive than greedy algorithms.

Markov chain Monte Carlo Model Composition (MC^3) (Raftery, Madigan, and Hoeting (1997)) uses MCMC to explore the model space. Typically MCMC is used to estimate the posterior of the parameters for a particular model. Thinking of the choice of model as the parameter of interest, MC^3 applies MCMC to find the posterior probabilities of the models. Analogous to ordinary MCMC, MC^3 simulates from a Markov chain with state space equal to the set of models under consideration and equilibrium distribution equal to the posterior probabilities of the models. Thus the proportion of time that the chain spends visiting each model is a simulation-consistent estimate of the posterior probability of that model. To create such a chain, let the transition probabilities between two models be as follows:

1. The probability of moving from the current model to a model which differs by two or more parameters (differing by inclusion or exclusion) is zero.

2. The probability of moving from the current model to one which differs by exactly one variable or node (either one more or one less) is $\min\{1, \frac{P(M'|D)}{P(M|D)}\}$, where $P(M'|D)$ is the posterior probability of the new model being considered, and $P(M|D)$ is the posterior distribution of the current model.

3. Otherwise, the chain stays in its current state.

For simpler models, such as linear regression, $P(M'|D)/P(M|D)$ can be found analytically. For neural networks, an approximation is necessary, and the BIC is again a convenient choice because of its relative ease of computation.

This algorithm has a feature which is potentially both a drawback and a benefit—it may visit the same model repeatedly. One could either keep track of all models visited or recompute the model each time. While it may be a waste of computing power to recompute the model after it has already been fit before, it is difficult to know for sure if the optimal fit has been found for a particular model, as mentioned above. Allowing the algorithm to refit each model when it is revisited and keeping only the best fit will make it more robust to these difficulties. Since the Markov chain will tend to spend more of its time around the models with highest posterior probability, it can thus spend more time making sure it has fit these models optimally and not worry about optimal fits for models that do not match the data well. In this way, MC^3 is another improvement over greedy algorithms such as stepwise and Occam's Window when dealing with neural networks.

Bayesian random searching (BARS) (Lee (2001)) attempts to improve upon MC^3 by removing a level of approximation. While MC^3 may be simulation-consistent, there have not been any studies done on how long the simulation needs to run in order to reach its equilibrium state. Furthermore, the estimates of the model probabilities (e.g., BICs) of the models visited are computed but not used directly in the final estimation of posterior probabilities. It seems wasteful to throw this information away and rely solely on the steady state properties of the chain. Instead, one can use the same Markov chain simulation but keep a record of the BIC or other Bayes factor estimates for all of the models visited. At the end of the Markov chain simulation, these estimates are then used directly to compute the posterior probabilities of the models. In practice, this may be more accurate than MC^3 because it does not rely on any of the steady state properties of the chain, removing a source of estimation error while retaining the advantages of an MCMC-based search. The chain is merely used as a mechanism for efficiently exploring the large model space, as the Markov chain should visit all models with relatively high posterior probability. This approach is similar to that of Chipman, George, and McCulloch (1998) in their implementation of Bayesian CART. Another shared advantage with MC^3 is that implementations of BARS for neural networks can refit models when they are revisited so that optimal model fitting is less of an issue.

4.2.3   Reversible Jump Markov Chain Monte Carlo

Reversible jump Markov chain Monte Carlo (RJMCMC) (Green (1995)) goes a level beyond MC^3, in that it attempts to simultaneously fit the model parameters and choose the size of the model. A single Markov chain traverses the joint space of models and parameters within models, using a generalization of the Metropolis–Hastings algorithm. In addition to steps which propose standard updates for values of parameters, steps can also propose adding or removing parameters from the model. For these model-changing steps (often referred to as birth and death steps), an additional term must be added to the probability of acceptance (α in Section 3.5) to account for the change in dimension of the parameter space. Thus a single chain is run, and one can use a sample from the steady-state distribution of the chain for estimating model probabilities (the proportion of time the chain spends visiting each model), for estimating the posterior for parameters of a particular model (treating the subset of draws for that model as an ordinary MCMC sample for that model), or for model averaging (averaging the predictions from each sample of the chain).

In practice, it can be difficult to make good proposals for births and deaths, because the parameters are highly correlated with each other, so adding or removing one tends to affect the values of all of the others. This is a particular problem for neural networks. Rios Insua and Müller (1998) give an algorithm for RJMCMC for moving between neural networks with different numbers of basis functions but for a fixed set of covariates. Their algorithm breaks each RJMCMC iteration into five steps: (i) standard Metropolis–Hastings updates for each γ_{jh}, (ii) a standard birth/death step for adding or removing a basis function, (iii) a seeding/thinning step that proposes adding (seeding) a new basis function by replicating a current γ_j and adding random noise, which is meant to help produce reasonable new values (or the matching thinning step which removes a random basis), (iv) a standard multivariate Gibbs update of β, and (v) standard Gibbs updates of all hyperparameters from their complete conditional distributions. They demonstrate reasonable movement of the chain between models using this algorithm. It appears that RJMCMC over the space of possible explanatory variables is considerably more difficult.

4.3 Ozone Data Analysis

We now return for a full analysis of the groundlevel ozone data introduced in Section 1.3. Overfitting would clearly be an issue with the highly correlated explanatory variables, so the model search methods of Sections 4.2.1 and 4.2.2 were applied, also searching over models with different numbers of basis functions. The flat prior of Section 3.3 was used here, although any of the other priors in this book could be substituted (those with substantially more shrinkage will result in different optimal models). For estimating relative model probabilities within the algorithms, the BIC approximation of Section 4.1.3 was used. The prior on the model space was taken to be flat (all models having equal prior probability).

All four of the algorithms generally found that the model with nearly all of the posterior probability was one with three nodes and five variables (VH, HUM, DPG, IBT, DAY) having BIC 264. The next best models were one with six nodes and five variables (HUM, DPG, IBT, VIS, DAY) having BIC 260, and one with three nodes and three variables (HUM, IBT, DAY) having BIC 259. Converting to the probability scale, these models were estimated to have posterior probabilities of approximately 97%, 2%, and 1%, respectively. On some runs, the stepwise algorithm and the Occam's Window algorithm would get stuck in a local maximum of the BIC and not find the global maximum, underscoring the importance of running those algorithms with several different starting models. The MCMC-based algorithms (BARS and MC^3) did not have this problem and could typically find the global maximum. Note that because a single model has almost all of the posterior probability, there is little difference between choosing the best model and doing full model averaging here.

It is somewhat difficult to display the fitted values for five independent variables simultaneously. Figure 4.3 shows fitted values (the solid line) plotted against the day of the year. However, unlike the fits from a model with only day as an explanatory variable (cf. Figures 4.1 and 4.2), the five-variable model fit is not a smooth curve when plotted against day because it also depends on the values of the other variables. However, one can still see that predicted ozone levels are generally higher in the summer (the middle of the year) relative to the other seasons. Similarly, plots of fitted values against the other explanatory variables (Figure 4.4) show nonsmooth marginal behavior but with clear overall trends.

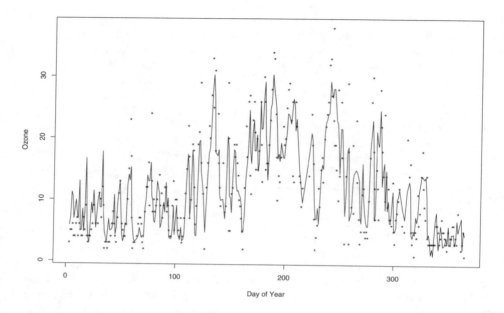

Day of Year

Figure 4.3. *Fitted ozone values (solid line) displayed marginally by day of year.*

One useful goodness-of-fit plot is to compare fitted values to actual observed ozone levels, as in Figure 4.5. It is clear that the model fits reasonably well, although there is a fair amount of unexplained variability left in the data.

This dataset has been analyzed by others in the nonparametric regression literature, and so it is useful for comparing neural network models to other nonparametric regression techniques. Breiman and Friedman (1985) used this dataset in their paper on alternating conditional expectation (ACE), which is a generalization of a GAM model (as in Section 2.1.1) that allows transformations of the response variable, with the direct goal of minimizing the mean-squared error. As a goodness-of-fit measure, they used the estimated multiple correlation coefficient, R^2. They fit the model using all nine explanatory variables, as well as a subset of only four that were chosen via a stepwise algorithm (the four are TEMP, IBH, DPG, and VIS). The comparison of the R^2's is shown in Table 4.1. Hastie and Tibshirani (1984) fit a standard GAM to the data. Friedman and Silverman (1989) fit the data using TURBO, a GAM that adaptively selects the spline knots and amount of smoothing. In the discussion of the previous paper, Hawkins (1989) fit the data with linear regression after using Box–Tidwell style transformations on the variables. For comparison, the neural network model with three nodes and five explanatory variables is also included. Table 4.1 shows that all of the above methods have similar goodness-of-fit to the data. All of the methods do manage to find a reasonable fit, but none is clearly better than the others.

Aside from the ACE model with only four variables, the other models in Table 4.1 all use more explanatory variables than does the neural network and are thus less parsimonious

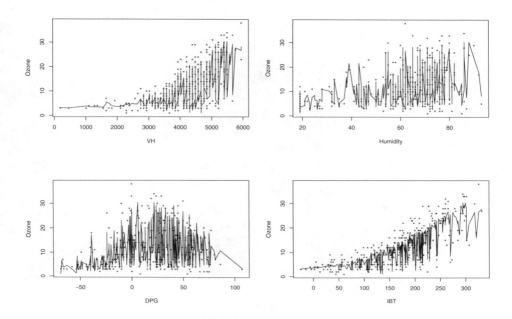

Figure 4.4. *Fitted ozone values (solid lines) displayed marginally by vertical height, humidity, pressure gradient, and inversion base temperature.*

and subject to increased prediction error. Hastie and Tibshirani (1990) do a comparison of several methods on these data in terms of variable selection. In addition to some of the above methods, they also include a stepwise algorithm for their GAM models, as well as a response to TURBO which they call BRUTO, which is another GAM extension, this one meant to do automatic variable and smoothing parameter selection. Table 4.2 shows the variables chosen by the models in each of these methods. It is interesting to note that the methods seriously disagree on which variables to select. Partly, this may be because the variables are highly correlated with each other (recall Figure 1.1) so that different subsets may give similar predictions. However, TURBO and BRUTO are largely in agreement with each other. And the three neural network models have similar choices of variables, although these are very different from those of TURBO and BRUTO. At the very least, it does seem clear that some variable selection is necessary because of the high level of correlation between the explanatory variables, even if there is dissent about which subset is optimal.

4.4   Loan Data Analysis

As an example of nonparametric classification, we now look at the loan applications data introduced in Section 1.4. Using a flat prior and a training set of 4000 observations, BARS (under the same setup as in the previous section) finds that the optimal model uses seven explanatory variables and two hidden nodes, and no other model has any significant pos-

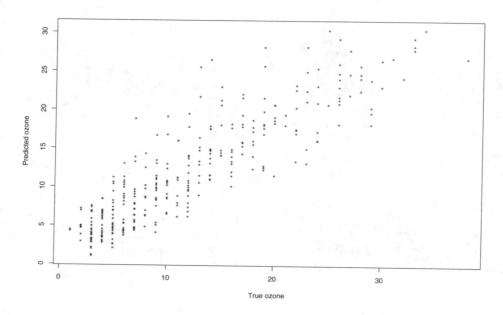

Figure 4.5. *Fitted ozone values by actual recorded levels.*

Table 4.1. *Comparison of fit of methods on the ozone data.*

Method	R^2
ACE, 9 variables	0.82
ACE, 4 variables	0.78
GAM	0.80
TURBO	0.80
Box–Tidwell	0.82
Neural Network	0.79

terior probability. The important variables are income, budgeted expenses, age, length of time at current residence, checking accounts with this bank, accounts at finance companies (typically these companies service customers who have trouble getting loans from standard banks and savings and loans), and category of loan. These are all reasonable variables, and collectively they seem to cover most of the important aspects of the covariates without much repetition, thus reducing the multicollinearity problems. This model has an error rate of 31% on the test data, which is not especially good, but, as described in Section 1.4, no model will be able to fit that well. It is helpful to recall that one of the primary goals of the analysis is model selection, in order to reduce the length of the application form. If a particular variable does not help with prediction, then it is likely that the bank does not need it on the application form.

Table 4.2. *Comparison of variable selection on the ozone data.*

Method	VH	WIND	HUM	TEMP	IBH	DPG	IBT	VIS	DAY
Stepwise ACE				X	X	X		X	
Stepwise GAM	X	X	X	X	X	X		X	X
TURBO	X			X	X	X		X	X
BRUTO				X	X	X		X	X
Best Neural Net (3 Nodes)	X		X			X	X		X
Second-best NN (6 Nodes)			X			X	X	X	X
Third-best NN (3 Nodes)			X				X		X

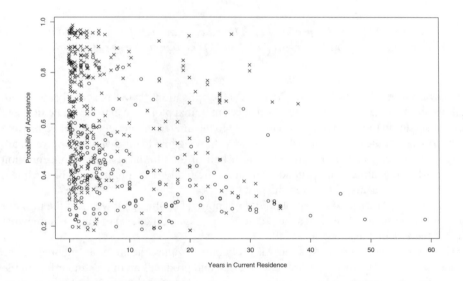

Figure 4.6. *Predicted probability of loan acceptance by length of time in current residence. An "x" marks a loan that was actually approved and an "O" a loan that was actually denied.*

Figure 4.6 shows the fitted probability that a loan was approved plotted against the length of time in years that the applicant had lived in their current residence (a stability variable) for a subsample of 500 points (using the whole dataset gives too cluttered a plot and

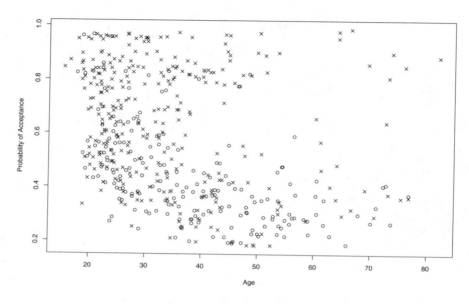

Figure 4.7. *Predicted probability of loan acceptance by age of applicant. An "x" marks a loan that was actually approved and an "O" a loan that was actually denied.*

is less informative). Points denoted with an "x" are applications that were actually approved, and those marked "O" were declined. As this is a marginal plot from a multivariate fit, there is a lot of scatter in the predictions, as compared to the univariate model in Figure 2.6. Note that the top half of the plot has mostly "x" marks showing that loans that were approved are generally predicted to be approved. The lower half of the plot has a higher concentration of "O" marks, indicating that declined loans are more likely to be predicted to be declined. The high error rate is also evident in the plot.

Figure 4.7 shows predicted probability of approval by the age in years of the primary applicant for the same 500 cases as the previous plot. Again, the level of noise is somewhat high, but the model does generally well.

Figure 4.8 plots predicted approval probability against the monthly income of the primary applicant. The income variable is skewed and produces an interesting effect in the plot. Oddly, people with higher incomes seem to be predicted to have lower probabilities of getting their loan approved. This phenomenon may be occurring because higher income people who are applying for unsecured personal loans tend to be people with other large debts, and so there is a worry that these people are taking on too much debt and spending beyond their means. Higher income people with better credit histories may tend to take out only secured loans (such as mortgages and car loans) rather than the unsecured loans which are the subject of this dataset.

This dataset was first analyzed with logistic regression, where model selection found that the best logistic regression models use 10–12 covariates and have error rates of around

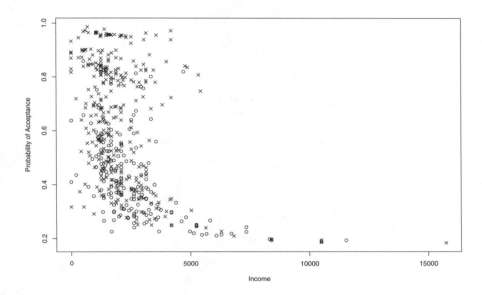

Figure 4.8. *Predicted probability of loan acceptance by monthly income of applicant. An "x" marks a loan that was actually approved and an "O" a loan that was actually denied.*

35% (Lee (2001)). For comparison, CART (introduced in Section 2.1.1) achieves an error rate of 31% and does so using the same variables found by BARS for a neural network model, although it also leaves out the number of checking accounts at the bank, doing even better at reducing the number of covariates. The flexibility of nonparametric methods such as CART or neural networks is clearly needed in order to minimize the number of covariates needed while still predicting as well as possible.

As another example, the model of Neal (1996) from Section 3.2 was fit with ARD (Section 4.1.6) using Neal's software, which is publicly available at

```
http://www.cs.utoronto.ca/~radford/fbm.software.html
```

A model with 20 basis functions appears to fit best and gives a 29% error rate on the test set. In this particular case, the fit is a little better than any of the previous models discussed (in general, the various flavors of neural networks, as well as many other nonparametric regression techniques, will give fairly similar results when used correctly). However, this better fit would be less helpful to the bank, which would not be able to reduce the application form as easily.

Chapter 5
Conclusions

Neural networks are best viewed as one tool in a large toolbox. A standard toolbox contains a number of different tools, because some are more appropriate than others for particular situations. You could use the handle end of a screwdriver to pound in a nail, but a hammer would work much better. On the other hand, a hammer would be less useful for a screw. The previous chapters have shown how neural networks fit as statistical models and how they belong in the nonparametric statistical toolbox. At this point, let us discuss some generalizations about the advantages and disadvantages of neural network models so that the best tool can be selected for the job.

Advantages:

- **Flexibility**—neural networks can approximate any reasonably behaved function with arbitrary accuracy, so one is not constrained to a particular parametric family and does not have to worry if the functional part of the model is correctly specified

- **High-dimensional**—neural networks are good for capturing high-dimensional effects, such as interactions between more than two explanatory variables, which can be quite difficult for parametric models to handle

- **Good track record**—neural network models have been used quite successfully in a wide variety of applications, as seen in both the scientific literature and by the sheer number of commercial software packages touting their algorithms

Disadvantages:

- **Complexity**—a larger number of parameters to be fit than a typical parametric model, and some of them can be difficult to fit

- **Lack of interpretability**—many of the parameters have no obvious interpretation, and the predicted values appear as if out of a black box

- **Difficult to specify prior information**—because the parameters lack clear interpretations, putting any meaningful information into the prior is not feasible

- **Convergence issues**—the likelihood and posterior surface tend to have many local maxima, and it is easy for fitting algorithms to become stuck without finding the global maximum or effectively exploring the full posterior surface

This list suggests a range of applications for which a neural network would be a poor choice. For example, if one believes that the data follow a particular parametric form, then that model should be used in favor of a neural network, which would be introducing unnecessary complexity (if one is not sure, a useful exercise is to try both and compare the results, preferring a simpler model when possible). In some cases, such as medical diagnosis, there is a preference for being able to understand how predictions relate to the explanatory variables, and a more intuitive structure (such as a tree) would be more appropriate. If prior information is available, a different nonparametric method that better allows incorporation of this information should be used. Even though a neural network is capable of fitting most data well, these examples illustrate a variety of cases where the practitioner should use a model other than a neural network.

On the flip side, neural network models are an obvious choice for a problem with little prior knowledge, with little information about the possible form of the fit, and with the possibility of higher-level interactions between covariates. This setup is a typical one in a data mining problem, for example. As datasets become more complex, the need for powerful tools such as neural networks will continue to grow. Their theoretical flexibility and good performance in practice make them highly useful.

Finally, a reminder that as neural networks are models, the standard modeling rules still apply. For example, models should be checked for fit and lack-of-fit. The tendency to treat a neural network as a magical black box often leads people to forget everything they have learned about fitting models and assume that the neural network will solve all their problems. Neural networks are a powerful tool, but they are only a tool and they still need to be used correctly.

Appendix A

Reference Prior Derivation

Here we follow the steps in Section 2 of Berger and Bernardo (1992) in the context of a neural network regression model, in order to compute something like a reference prior. The notation here also follows that paper. The first key decision to make is that of an ordering and partitioning scheme for the parameters, with the idea that the key parameters are listed in order of importance, with nuisance parameters at the end. For a neural network, as with most regression problems, the precision, τ, is typically seen as a nuisance parameter, and it is thus listed last. The γ_{jh} parameters appearing inside the logistic basis functions are the most difficult to deal with in choosing a prior, so they are listed first, leaving the β linear coefficients in between γ and τ (this also makes the computations more tractable). Thus our parameter vector is partitioned into three groups: $\theta = (\theta_1, \theta_2, \theta_3) = (\gamma, \beta, \tau)$ as in Chapter 3. Define $\theta_{[j]} = (\theta_1, \ldots, \theta_j)$ and $\theta_{[\sim j]} = (\theta_{j+1}, \ldots, \theta_3)$, e.g., $\theta_{[2]} = (\gamma, \beta)$ and $\theta_{[\sim 2]} = \tau$. By convention, $\theta_{[0]}$ is empty and $\theta_{[\sim 0]} = \theta$. Denote the universe of possible values of θ by Θ.

Step 1 is to choose a nested sequence $\{\Theta^l\}$ of compact subsets of Θ such that their infinite union is the universe. Here we take

$$\Theta^l = \left(-\frac{l}{2}, \frac{l}{2}\right)^{k(r+1)} \times \left(-\frac{l}{2}, \frac{l}{2}\right)^{k+1} \times \left(\frac{1}{l}, l\right).$$

Define $\Theta^l(\theta_{[j]}) = \{\theta_{j+1} : (\theta_{[j]}, \theta_{j+1}, \theta_{[\sim(j+1)]}) \in \Theta^l \text{ for some } \theta_{[\sim(j+1)]}\}$. Denote the indicator function $1_{\Theta}(\theta) = 1$ if $\theta \in \Theta$ and 0 otherwise. To reduce notational clutter, define
$1_{\Theta^l(\theta_{[j]})}(\theta_{j+1}, \ldots, \theta_{j+h}) = \prod_{i=1}^{h} 1_{\Theta^l(\theta_{[j+i-1]})}(\theta_{j+i})$.

Step 2 is the ordering and partitioning, which was done above.

Step 3 is the actual computation of the reference prior, which requires some additional notation. Let $I(\theta)$ be the Fisher information matrix, as in equation (3.6). Let $S = S(\theta) = (I(\theta))^{-1}$ be its inverse. Partition S into three parts corresponding to γ, β, and τ, just as θ is partitioned, and denote the blocks by A_{ij}:

$$S = \begin{bmatrix} A_{11} & A_{21}^t & A_{31}^t \\ A_{21} & A_{22} & A_{32}^t \\ A_{31} & A_{32} & A_{33} \end{bmatrix}.$$

81

Now define S_j to be the upper-left j-block of S, i.e.,

$$S_j = \begin{bmatrix} A_{11} & \cdots & \\ \vdots & \ddots & \\ & & A_{jj} \end{bmatrix},$$

for $j \in \{1, 2, 3\}$. Let $H_j = S_j^{-1}$ and h_j be the lower right block of H_j. What does all this mean in terms of our neural network model? First,

$$S = \begin{bmatrix} \frac{1}{\tau} \begin{bmatrix} \tau \mathbf{G'G} & \tau \mathbf{G'\Gamma} \\ \tau \mathbf{\Gamma'G} & \tau \mathbf{\Gamma'\Gamma} \end{bmatrix}^{-1} & 0 \\ & 0 \\ 0 \quad 0 & \frac{2\tau^2}{n} \end{bmatrix}.$$

That upper left block can be computed using formulae for inverting partitioned matrices (in many linear algebra and linear models books). The only piece we actually need to compute is the extreme corner, $A_{11} = \frac{1}{\tau}\left(\mathbf{G'G} - \mathbf{G'\Gamma}(\mathbf{\Gamma'\Gamma})^{-1}\mathbf{\Gamma'G}\right)^{-1}$, which gives us $h_1 = A_{11}^{-1} = \tau \mathbf{G'}(\mathbf{I} - \mathbf{\Gamma}(\mathbf{\Gamma'\Gamma})^{-1}\mathbf{\Gamma'})\mathbf{G}$. It is much simpler to see that $h_2 = \tau \mathbf{\Gamma'\Gamma}$ and $h_3 = \frac{n}{2\tau^2}$.

The prior is computed iteratively, starting with the least important parameters. Start by defining

$$\pi_3^l(\boldsymbol{\theta}_{[\sim 2]}|\boldsymbol{\theta}_{[2]}) = \pi_3^l(\tau|\boldsymbol{\gamma}, \boldsymbol{\beta}) = \frac{|h_3(\boldsymbol{\theta})|^{1/2} 1_{\boldsymbol{\Theta}^l(\boldsymbol{\theta}_{[2]})}(\theta_3)}{\int_{\boldsymbol{\Theta}^l(\boldsymbol{\theta}_{[2]})} |h_3(\boldsymbol{\theta})|^{1/2} d\theta_3}$$

$$= \frac{\frac{1}{\tau} 1_{\boldsymbol{\Theta}^l(\boldsymbol{\gamma}, \boldsymbol{\beta})}(\tau)}{\int_{1/l}^l \frac{1}{\tau} d\tau}$$

$$= \frac{1}{\tau}\frac{1}{2\log l} 1_{\boldsymbol{\Theta}^l(\boldsymbol{\gamma}, \boldsymbol{\beta})}(\tau).$$

Now for $j = 2$ and $j = 1$, define

$$\pi_j^l(\boldsymbol{\theta}_{[\sim(j-1)]}|\boldsymbol{\theta}_{[j-1]}) = \frac{\pi_{j+1}^l(\boldsymbol{\theta}_{[\sim j]}|\boldsymbol{\theta}_{[j]}) \exp\left\{\frac{1}{2}E_j^l\left[(\log |h_j(\boldsymbol{\theta})|)|\boldsymbol{\theta}_{[j]}\right]\right\} 1_{\boldsymbol{\Theta}^l(\boldsymbol{\theta}_{[j-1]})}(\theta_j)}{\int_{\boldsymbol{\Theta}^l(\boldsymbol{\theta}_{[j-1]})} \exp\left\{\frac{1}{2}E_j^l\left[(\log |h_j(\boldsymbol{\theta})|)|\boldsymbol{\theta}_{[j]}\right]\right\} d\theta_j},$$

where

$$E_j^l\left[g(\boldsymbol{\theta})|\boldsymbol{\theta}_{[j]}\right] = \int_{\{\boldsymbol{\theta}_{[\sim j]}:(\boldsymbol{\theta}_{[j]}, \boldsymbol{\theta}_{[\sim j]})\in\boldsymbol{\Theta}^l\}} g(\boldsymbol{\theta})\pi_{j+1}^l(\boldsymbol{\theta}_{[\sim j]}|\boldsymbol{\theta}_{[j]}) d\boldsymbol{\theta}_{[\sim j]}.$$

Direct calculation shows that

$$E_2^l\left[(\log |h_2(\boldsymbol{\theta})|)|\boldsymbol{\gamma}, \boldsymbol{\beta}\right] = (k + 1)\log |\mathbf{\Gamma'\Gamma}|$$

$$\pi_2^l(\boldsymbol{\beta}, \tau|\boldsymbol{\gamma}) = \frac{\frac{1}{2\tau \log l} \exp\left\{\frac{k+1}{2}\log |\mathbf{\Gamma'\Gamma}|\right\} 1_{\boldsymbol{\Theta}^l(\boldsymbol{\gamma})}(\boldsymbol{\beta}, \tau)}{\int_{\boldsymbol{\Theta}^l(\boldsymbol{\gamma})} \exp\left\{\frac{k+1}{2}\log |\mathbf{\Gamma'\Gamma}|\right\} d\boldsymbol{\beta}}$$

$$= \frac{1_{\Theta^l(\gamma)}(\beta, \tau)}{2\tau \log l \int_{\Theta^l(\gamma)} d\beta} = \frac{1}{2\tau l^{k+1} \log l} 1_{\Theta^l(\gamma)}(\beta, \tau)$$

$$E_1^l\left[(\log|h_1(\theta)|)|\,\gamma\right] = \int_{\left\{\beta,\tau:\theta\in\Theta^l\right\}} \left(\log|G^t(I - \Gamma(\Gamma^t\Gamma)^{-1}\Gamma^t)G|\right.$$

$$\left. + k(r+1)\log\tau\right) \frac{1}{2\tau l^{k+1}\log l} d\beta d\tau$$

$$= \int_{\left\{\beta:\theta\in\Theta^l\right\}} \log|G^t(I - \Gamma(\Gamma^t\Gamma)^{-1}\Gamma^t)G| l^{-(k+1)} d\beta.$$

To simplify the equations, we introduce a little more notation. Let $H = F^t RF$, where $R = I - \Gamma(\Gamma^t\Gamma)^{-1}\Gamma^t$ and F is the matrix G with all of the β terms removed; i.e., F has elements $f_{ij} = x_{ih}\Gamma_{ig}(1 - \Gamma_{ig})$, where g is the integer part of $\frac{j}{r+1}$ and h is the remainder (cf. equation (3.5)). Thus we can now write

$$|G^t(I - \Gamma(\Gamma^t\Gamma)^{-1}\Gamma^t)G| = |F^t RF| \prod_{j=1}^k \beta_j^{2(r+1)} = |H| \prod_{j=1}^k \beta_j^{2(r+1)}.$$

Continuing with the prior calculations,

$$E_1^l\left[(\log|h_1(\theta)|)|\,\gamma\right] = \int_{\left\{\beta:\theta\in\Theta^l\right\}} l^{-(k+1)} \log\left(|H| \prod_{j=1}^k \beta_j^{2(r+1)}\right) d\beta$$

$$= \log|H| + \int_{\left\{\beta:\theta\in\Theta^l\right\}} \frac{r+1}{l^{k+1}} \sum_{j=1}^k \log\beta_j^2 \, d\beta$$

$$= \log|H| + \sum_{j=1}^k \frac{r+1}{l^{k+1}} \int_{-l/2}^{l/2} \log\beta_j^2 \, d\beta_j$$

$$= \log|H| + \frac{2k(r+1)}{l^k}\left(\log\frac{l}{2} - 1\right),$$

$$\pi_1^l(\theta) = \frac{\frac{1}{2\tau l^{k+1}\log l} \exp\left\{\frac{1}{2}\left[\log|H| + 2k(r+1)\left(\log\frac{l}{2} - 1\right)/l^k\right]\right\} 1_{\Theta^l}(\theta)}{\int_{\Theta^l(\theta_{[0]})} \exp\left\{\frac{1}{2}\left[\log|H| + 2k(r+1)\left(\log\frac{l}{2} - 1\right)/l^k\right]\right\} d\gamma}$$

$$= \frac{|H|^{1/2} 1_{\Theta^l}(\theta)}{2\tau l^{k+1}\log l \int_{\Theta^l(\theta_{[0]})} |H|^{1/2} d\gamma}.$$

Finally, let θ^* be any fixed point with positive density for all π_1^l. A reference prior is given by

$$\pi(\theta) = \lim_{l\to\infty} \frac{\pi_1^l(\theta)}{\pi_1^l(\theta^*)} \propto \frac{1}{\tau}|H|^{1/2}.$$

Unfortunately, like the other noninformative priors of Section 3.3, this reference prior also leads to an improper posterior, and so to be viable, the parameter space must be appropriately truncated, as with the other priors in Section 3.3.

Glossary

activation function a function used as the basis set for a neural network; historically these were indicator functions, but now they are sigmoidal functions

artificial neural network a neural network used as a statistical model, as distinguished from a model of a biological process for thought

backpropagation a gradient descent algorithm for fitting neural network parameters that takes advantage of the structure of the model

bias an intercept parameter for a neural network (of course, it can also mean the difference between the expected value of an estimator and the true value of what it is trying to estimate)

feature explanatory variable

feature selection variable selection

feed forward predicted values are an explicit function of explanatory variables, as opposed to a network with cycles (feedback) which allow only an implicit representation of predictions

Heaviside function an indicator function that takes value one when its argument is true and value zero when its argument is false

hidden node logistic basis function

input explanatory variable

neural network a statistical model that uses logistic basis functions

output fitted value for a response variable

perceptron a hidden node in a neural network; historically these were indicator functions used as basis functions, but the term is now sometimes applied to logistic basis functions, usually in the phrase "multilayer perceptron" (which is just a standard neural network)

radial basis network a mixture model, typically of normals with equal variance, interpreted as a network structure analogous to a neural network

sigmoidal function a monotone function with lower and upper asymptotes and a smooth rise between, which looks vaguely "S" shaped; for a neural network, this is typically either a logistic or a hyperbolic tangent

softmax function transforms a set of real numbers to probabilities by exponentiating each of them and then dividing by the sum of all of the exponentiated values

supervised learning standard training a model or algorithm to fit one or more response variables using a set of explanatory variables

test dataset a subset of the data not used during model fitting and then used to validate predicted values, a sort of simplified cross-validation; cf. training data set

threshold function indicator function; cf. Heaviside function

training dataset a subset of the data used to fit the parameters of the model; cf. test data set

unsupervised learning fitting a model or algorithm without an observed response variable, for example clustering

weights the (nonvariance) parameters of a neural network

Bibliography

Abramowitz, M. and Stegun, I. A., eds. (1965). *Handbook of Mathematical Functions*. New York: Dover Publications.

Akaike, H. (1974). "A New Look at Statistical Model Identification." *IEEE Transactions on Automatic Control*, AU–19, 716–722.

Anderson, J. A. (1982). "Logistic Discrimination." In *Classification, Pattern Recognition and Reduction of Dimensionality*, eds. P. R. Krishnaiah and L. N. Kanal, Vol. 2 of *Handbook of Statistics*, 169–191. Amsterdam: North–Holland.

Andrieu, C., de Freitas, J. F. G., and Doucet, A. (2001). "Robust Full Bayesian Learning for Radial Basis Networks." *Neural Computation*, 13, 2359–2407.

Barbieri, M. M. and Berger, J. O. (2002). "Optimal Predictive Model Selection." Tech. Rep. 02-02, Duke University, ISDS.

Barron, A., Schervish, M. J., and Wasserman, L. (1999). "The Consistency of Posterior Distributions in Nonparametric Problems." *Annals of Statistics*, 27, 536–561.

Berger, J. O. and Bernardo, J. M. (1992). "On the Development of Reference Priors." In *Bayesian Statistics* 4, eds. J. M. Bernardo, J. O. Berger, A. P. Dawid, and A. F. M. Smith, 35–60. New York: Oxford University Press.

Berger, J. O., De Oliveira, V., and Sansó, B. (2001). "Objective Bayesian Analysis of Spatially Correlated Data." *Journal of the American Statistical Association*, 96, 1361–1374.

Berger, J. O. and Pericchi, L. R. (1996). "The Intrinsic Bayes Factor for Model Selection and Prediction." *Journal of the American Statistical Association*, 91, 109–122.

Bernardo, J. M. (1979). "Reference Posterior Distributions for Bayesian Inference (with discussion)." *Journal of the Royal Statistical Society Series B*, 41, 113–147.

Bernardo, J. M. and Smith, A. F. M. (1994). *Bayesian Theory*. Chichester: John Wiley & Sons.

Bishop, C. M. (1995). *Neural Networks for Pattern Recognition*. Oxford: Clarendon Press.

87

Breiman, L. (1994). "Heuristics of Instability in Model Selection." Tech. Rep., University of California at Berkeley.

Breiman, L. (1996). "Bagging Predictors." *Machine Learning*, 26, 123–140.

Breiman, L. and Friedman, J. H. (1985). "Estimating Optimal Transformations for Multiple Regression and Correlation." *Journal of the American Statistical Association*, 80, 580–619.

Breiman, L., Friedman, J. H., Olshen, R., and Stone, C. (1984). *Classification and Regression Trees*. Belmont, CA: Wadsworth.

Bridle, J. S. (1989). "Probabilistic Interpretation of Feedforward Classification Network Outputs, with Relationships to Statistical Pattern Recognition." In *Neuro-computing: Algorithms, Architectures and Applications*, eds. F. F. Soulié and J. Héault, 227–236. New York: Springer-Verlag.

Bühlmann, P. and Yu, B. (2002). "Analyzing Bagging." *Annals of Statistics*, 30, 927–961.

Buntine, W. L. and Weigend, A. S. (1991). "Bayesian Back-Propagation." *Complex Systems*, 5, 603–643.

Carlin, B. P. and Louis, T. A. (2000). *Bayes and Empirical Bayes Methods for Data Analysis*. Boca Raton, FL: Chapman & Hall/CRC.

Cheng, B. and Titterington, D. M. (1994). "Neural Networks: A Review from a Statistical Perspective." *Statistical Science*, 9, 2–30.

Chipman, H., George, E., and McCulloch, R. (1998). "Bayesian CART Model Search (with discussion)." *Journal of the American Statistical Association*, 93, 935–960.

Chipman, H. A., George, E. I., and McCulloch, R. E. (2002). "Bayesian Treed Models." *Machine Learning*, 48, 303–324.

Chui, C. K. (1988). *Multivariate Splines*. CBMS-NSF Regional Conf. Ser. in Appl. Math. 54. Philadelphia: SIAM.

Cleveland, W. S. (1979). "Robust Locally-Weighted Regression and Smoothing Scatterplots." *Journal of the American Statistical Association*, 74, 829–836.

Clyde, M. A. (1999). "Bayesian Model Averaging and Model Search Strategies (with discussion)." In *Bayesian Statistics* 6, eds. J. M. Bernardo, J. O. Berger, A. P. Dawid, and A. F. M. Smith, 157–185. New York: Oxford University Press.

Clyde, M. A. and Lee, H. K. H. (2001). "Bagging and the Bayesian Bootstrap." In *Artificial Intelligence and Statistics* 2001, eds. T. Richardson and T. Jaakkola, 169–174. San Francisco: Morgan Kaufmann.

Congdon, P. (2001). *Bayesian Statistical Modelling*. New York: John Wiley & Sons.

Craig, B. (1997). "Manatee: Selecting from Among Several Models." Presented at 1997 Joint Statistical Meetings, Anaheim, CA.

Cressie, N. A. C. (1991). *Statistics for Spatial Data*. New York: Wiley-Interscience.

Cybenko, G. (1989). "Approximation by Superpositions of a Sigmoidal Function." *Mathematics of Control, Signals and Systems*, 2, 303–314.

de Boor, C. (2002). *A Practical Guide to Splines*. Revised edition. New York: Springer-Verlag.

Denison, D. G. T., Holmes, C. C., Mallick, B. K., and Smith, A. F. M. (2002). *Bayesian Methods for Nonlinear Classification and Regression*. London: Wiley & Sons.

Denison, D. G. T., Mallick, B. K., and Smith, A. F. M. (1998a). "A Bayesian CART Algorithm." *Biometrika*, 85, 363–377.

Denison, D. G. T., Mallick, B. K., and Smith, A. F. M. (1998b). "Bayesian MARS." *Statistics and Computing*, 8, 337–346.

Diebolt, J. and Robert, C. (1994). "Estimation of Finite Mixture Distributions through Bayesian Sampling." *Journal of the Royal Statistical Society Series B*, 56, 363–375.

Draper, D. (1995). "Assessment and Propagation of Model Uncertainty." *Journal of the Royal Statistical Society Series B*, 57, 45–98.

Duda, R. O., Hart, P. E., and Stork, D. G. (2001). *Pattern Classification*. New York: John Wiley & Sons.

Epanechnikov, V. (1969). "Nonparametric Estimates of a Multivariate Probability Density." *Theory of Probability and its Applications*, 14, 153–158.

Evans, M. and Swartz, T. (1995). "Methods for Approximating Integrals in Statistics with Special Emphasis on Bayesian Integration Problems." *Statistical Science*, 10, 254–272.

Fine, T. L. (1999). *Feedforward Neural Network Methodology*. New York: Springer-Verlag.

French, S. and Rios Insua, D. (2000). *Statistical Decision Theory*. London: Edward Arnold.

Friedman, J. H. (1991). "Multivariate Adaptive Regression Splines." *Annals of Statistics*, 19, 1–141.

Friedman, J. H. and Silverman, B. W. (1989). "Flexible Parsimonious Smoothing and Additive Modelling (with discussion)." *Technometrics*, 31, 3–39.

Friedman, J. H. and Stuetzle, W. (1981). "Projection Pursuit Regression." *Journal of the American Statistical Association*, 76, 817–823.

Funahashi, K. (1989). "On the Approximate Realization of Continuous Mappings by Neural Networks." *Neural Networks*, 2, 183–192.

Gelfand, A. E. and Dey, D. K. (1994). "Bayesian Model Choice: Asymptotics and Exact Calculations." *Journal of the Royal Statistical Society Series B*, 56, 501–514.

Gelman, A., Carlin, J. B., Stern, H. S., and Rubin, D. B. (1995). *Bayesian Data Analysis*. London: Chapman and Hall.

Geman, S. and Geman, D. (1984). "Stochastic Relaxation, Gibbs Distributions and the Bayesian Restoration of Images." *IEEE Transactions on Pattern Analysis and Machine Intelligence*, 6, 721–741.

Gentle, J. E. (2002). *Elements of Computational Statistics*. New York: Springer-Verlag.

Geweke, J. (1989). "Bayesian Inference in Econometric Models Using Monte Carlo Integration." *Econometrica*, 57, 1317–1340.

Gibbs, M. N. and MacKay, D. J. C. (1997). "Efficient Implementation of Gaussian Processes." Tech. Rep., Cavendish Laboratory, Cambridge.

Gilks, W. R., Richardson, S., and Spiegelhalter, D. J. (1996). *Markov Chain Monte Carlo in Practice*. London: Chapman and Hall.

Gordon, A. D. (1999). *Classification*. Monogr. Statist. Appl. Probab. 82, 2nd ed. Boca Raton, FL: Chapman & Hall/CRC.

Green, P. J. (1995). "Reversible Jump Markov Chain Monte Carlo Computation and Bayesian Model Determination." *Biometrika*, 82, 711–732.

Green, P. J. and Silverman, B. W. (1994). *Nonparametric Regression and Generalized Linear Models: A Roughness Penalty Approach*. London: Chapman and Hall.

Grenander, U. (1981). *Abstract Inference*. New York: Wiley.

Härdle, W. (1990). *Applied Nonparametric Regression*. Cambridge, UK: Cambridge University Press.

Härdle, W. (1991). *Smoothing Techniques with Implementation in S*. New York: Springer-Verlag.

Hartigan, J. A. (1964). "Invariant Prior Distributions." *Annals of Mathematical Statistics*, 35, 836–845.

Hartigan, J. A. (1983). *Bayes Theory*. New York: Springer-Verlag.

Hastie, T. and Tibshirani, R. (1984). "Generalized Additive Models." Tech. Rep. 98, Stanford University, Department of Statistics.

Hastie, T. and Tibshirani, R. (1990). *Generalized Additive Models*. London: Chapman and Hall.

Hastie, T., Tibshirani, R., and Friedman, J. (2001). *The Elements of Statistical Learning*. New York: Springer-Verlag.

Hastings, W. K. (1970). "Monte Carlo Sampling Methods Using Markov Chains and Their Applications." *Biometrika*, 57, 97–109.

Hawkins, D. (1989). "Discussion of 'Flexible Parsimonious Smoothing and Additive Modelling' by J. Friedman and B. Silverman." *Technometrics*, 31, 3–39.

Hjort, N. L. and Omre, H. (1994). "Topics in Spatial Statistics." *Scandinavian Journal of Statistics*, 21, 289–357.

Hoeting, J. A., Madigan, D., Raftery, A. E., and Volinsky, C. T. (1999). "Bayesian Model Averaging: A Tutorial (with discussion)." *Statistical Science*, 14, 382–417.

Holmes, C. C. and Adams, N. M. (2002). "A Probabilistic Nearest Neighbour Method for Statistical Pattern Recognition." *Journal of the Royal Statistical Society Series B*, 64, 295–306.

Holmes, C. C. and Mallick, B. K. (1998). "Bayesian Radial Basis Functions of Variable Dimension." *Neural Computation*, 10, 1217–1233.

Holmes, C. C. and Mallick, B. K. (2000). "Bayesian Wavelet Networks for Nonparametric Regression." *IEEE Transactions on Neural Networks*, 11, 27–35.

Holmes, C. C. and Mallick, B. K. (2001). "Bayesian Regression with Multivariate Linear Splines." *Journal of the Royal Statistical Society Series B*, 63, 3–18.

Hornik, K., Stinchcombe, M., and White, H. (1989). "Multilayer Feedforward Networks are Universal Approximators." *Neural Networks*, 2, 359–366.

Jeffreys, H. (1946). "An Invariant Form for the Prior Probability in Estimation Problems." *Proceedings of the Royal Society London A*, 186, 453–461.

Jeffreys, H. (1961). *Theory of Probability*. 3rd ed. New York: Oxford University Press.

Kass, R. E. and Raftery, A. E. (1995). "Bayes Factors." *Journal of the American Statistical Association*, 90, 773–795.

Kass, R. E. and Wasserman, L. (1995). "A Reference Bayesian Test for Nested Hypotheses and Its Relationship to the Schwarz Criterion." *Journal of the American Statistical Association*, 90, 928–934.

Kass, R. E. and Wasserman, L. (1996). "The Selection of Prior Distributions by Formal Rules." *Journal of the American Statistical Association*, 91, 1343–1370.

Keribin, C. (2000). "Consistent Estimation of the Order of Mixture Models." *Sankhya*, 62, 49–66.

Leamer, E. E. (1978). *Specification Searches: Ad Hoc Inference with Nonexperimental Data*. New York: Wiley.

Lee, H. K. H. (2000). "Consistency of Posterior Distributions for Neural Networks." *Neural Networks*, 13, 629–642.

Lee, H. K. H. (2001). "Model Selection for Neural Network Classification." *Journal of Classification*, 18, 227–243.

Lee, H. K. H. (2002). "Difficulties in Estimating the Normalizing Constant of the Posterior for a Neural Network." *Journal of Computational and Graphical Statistics*, 11, 222–235.

Lee, H. K. H. (2003). "A Noninformative Prior for Neural Networks." *Machine Learning*, 50, 197–212.

Loader, C. (1999). *Local Regression and Likelihood*. New York: Springer-Verlag.

MacKay, D. J. C. (1992). "Bayesian Methods for Adaptive Methods." Ph.D. thesis, California Institute of Technology, Program in Computation and Neural Systems.

MacKay, D. J. C. (1994). "Bayesian Non-linear Modeling for the Energy Prediction Competition." *ASHRAE Transactions*, 100, pt. 2, 1053–1062.

McCullagh, P. and Nelder, J. A. (1983). *Generalized Linear Models*. London: Chapman and Hall.

McCulloch, W. S. and Pitts, W. (1943). "A Logical Calculus of the Ideas Imminent in Nervous Activity." *Bulletin of Mathematical Biophysics*, 5, 115–133.

Meng, X. L. and Wong, W. H. (1996). "Simulating Ratios of Normalizing Constants via a Simple Identity: A Theoretical Exploration." *Statistica Sinica*, 4, 831–860.

Metropolis, N., Rosenbluth, A. W., Rosenbluth, M. N., Teller, A. H., and Teller, E. (1953). "Equations of State Calculations by Fast Computing Machine." *Journal of Chemical Physics*, 21, 1087–1091.

Minsky, M. L. and Papert, S. A. (1969). *Perceptrons*. Cambridge, MA: MIT Press.

Müller, P. and Rios Insua, D. (1998). "Issues in Bayesian Analysis of Neural Network Models." *Neural Computation*, 10, 571–592.

Murata, N., Yoshizawa, S., and Amari, S. (1994). "Network Information Criterion—Determining the Number of Hidden Units for an Artificial Neural Network Model." *IEEE Transactions on Neural Networks*, 5, 6, 865–871.

Neal, R. M. (1996). *Bayesian Learning for Neural Networks*. New York: Springer-Verlag.

Neal, R. M. (1999). "Regression and Classification Using Gaussian Process Priors." In *Bayesian Statistics* 6, eds. J. M. Bernardo, J. O. Berger, A. P. Dawid, and A. F. M. Smith, 475–501. Oxford: Clarendon Press.

Ogden, R. T. (1997). *Essential Wavelets for Statistical Applications and Data Analysis*. Boston: Birkhäuser.

O'Hagan, A. (1978). "Curve Fitting and Optimal Design for Prediction." *Journal of the Royal Statistical Society Series B*, 40, 1–42.

O'Hagan, A. (1995). "Fractional Bayes Factors for Model Comparisons." *Journal of the Royal Statistical Society Series B*, 57, 99–138.

Press, S. J. (1989). *Bayesian Statistics: Principles, Models, and Applications*. New York: John Wiley & Sons.

Raftery, A. E. (1996). "Approximate Bayes Factors and Accounting for Model Uncertainty in Generalized Linear Models." *Biometrika*, 83, 251–266.

Raftery, A. E. and Madigan, D. (1994). "Model Selection and Accounting for Model Uncertainty in Graphical Models Using Occam's Window." *Journal of the American Statistical Association*, 89, 1535–1546.

Raftery, A. E., Madigan, D., and Hoeting, J. A. (1997). "Bayesian Model Averaging for Linear Regression Models." *Journal of the American Statistical Association*, 437, 179–191.

Rios Insua, D. and Müller, P. (1998). "Feedforward Neural Networks for Nonparametric Regression." In *Practical Nonparametric and Semiparametric Bayesian Statistics*, eds. D. Dey, P. Müller, and D. Sinha, 181–193. New York: Springer-Verlag.

Ripley, B. D. (1996). *Pattern Recognition and Neural Networks*. Cambridge, UK: Cambridge University Press.

Robert, C. P. (2001). *The Bayesian Choice: From Decision-Theoretic Foundations to Computational Implementation*. New York: Springer-Verlag.

Robert, C. P. and Casella, G. (2000). *Monte Carlo Statistical Methods*. New York: Springer-Verlag.

Robinson, M. (2001a). "Priors for Bayesian Neural Networks." Master's thesis, University of British Columbia, Department of Statistics.

Robinson, M. (2001b). "Priors for Bayesian Neural Networks." In *Computing Science and Statistics*, eds. E. J. Wegman, A. Braverman, A. Goodman, and P. Smyth, Vol. 33, 122–127.

Rosenblatt, F. (1962). *Principles of Neurodynamics: Perceptrons and the Theory of Brain Mechanisms*. Washington, D.C.: Spartan.

Rubin, D. B. (1981). "The Bayesian Bootstrap." *Annals of Statistics*, 9, 130–134.

Rumelhart, D. E., Hinton, G. E., and Williams, R. J. (1986). "Learning Internal Representations by Error Propagation." In *Parallel Distributed Processing: Explorations in the Microstructure of Cognition*, eds. D. E. Rumelhart, J. L. McClelland, and the PDP Research Group, Vol. 1, 318–362. Cambridge, MA: MIT Press.

Sarle, W. S. (1994). "Neural Network Implementation in SAS Software." In *Proceedings of the Nineteenth Annual SAS Users Group International Conference*, 38–51. SAS Institute, Cary, NC.

Schervish, M. J. (1995). *Theory of Statistics*. New York: Springer-Verlag.

Schwarz, G. (1978). "Estimating the Dimension of a Model." *Annals of Statistics*, 6, 461–464.

Silverman, B. W. (1985). "Some Aspects of the Spline Smoothing Approach to Nonparametric Curve Fitting." *Journal of the Royal Statistical Society Series B*, 47, 1–52.

Silverman, B. W. (1986). *Density Estimation for Statistics and Data Analysis*. London: Chapman and Hall.

Stern, H. S. (1996). "Neural Networks in Applied Statistics." *Technometrics*, 38, 205–214.

Tierney, L. and Kadane, J. (1986). "Accurate Approximations for Posterior Moments and Marginal Densities." *Journal of the American Statistical Association*, 81, 82–86.

Venables, W. N. and Ripley, B. D. (1999). *Modern Applied Statistics with S-PLUS*. 3rd ed. New York: Springer-Verlag.

Vidakovic, B. (1999). *Statistical Modeling by Wavelets*. New York: John Wiley & Sons.

Wahba, G. (1990). *Spline Models for Observational Data*. CBMS-NSF Regional Conf. Ser. in Appl. Math. 59. Philadelphia: SIAM.

Warner, B. and Misra, M. (1996). "Understanding Neural Networks as Statistical Tools." *American Statistician*, 50, 284–293.

Wasserman, L. (2000). "Asymptotic Inference for Mixture Models by Using Data-Dependent Priors." *Journal of the Royal Statistical Society Series B*, 62, 159–180.

Widrow, B. and Hoff, M. E. (1960). "Institute of Radio Engineers, Western Electronic Show and Convention, Convention Record." In *Adaptive Switching Circuits*, Vol. 4, 96–104. New York: Institute of Radio Engineers.

Williams, C. K. I. and Rasmussen, C. E. (1996). "Gaussian Processes for Regression." In *Advances in Neural Information Processing Systems* 8, eds. D. S. Tourestzky, M. C. Mozer, and M. E. Haeelmo. Cambridge, MA: MIT Press.

Wong, W. H. and Shen, X. (1995). "Probability Inequalities for Likelihood Ratios and Convergence Rates of Sieve MLEs." *Annals of Statistics*, 23, 339–362.

Index